CW00349325

Best of British
CHEESE

Rebecca King

**DIAL
HOUSE**

CONTENTS

First published 1995

ISBN 0 7110 2299 2

© Rebecca King 1995

Published by Dial House

an imprint of Ian Allan Ltd, Terminal House, Station Approach, Shepperton, Surrey TW17 8AS.

Printed by Ian Allan Printing Ltd, Coombelands House, Coombelands Lane, Addlestone, Weybridge, Surrey KT15 1HY.

The word STILTON is a Certification Trade Mark vested in the Stilton Cheesemaker's Association. The photograph on pages 4 and 5 was supplied by the SCMA.

Introduction

If a random selection of people were to be asked whether or not they like cheese, it is unlikely that there would be many negative answers.

Cheese, of course, means different things to different people: to some, it means sandwiches, to some, it means sandwiches, ploughman's lunches, cheese on toast, macaroni cheese, cauliflower cheese or fondues; to cooks it is an invaluable ingredient when preparing exciting dishes, vegetarian or otherwise; to others it means good table cheeses and the perfect way to end a meal.

Most people are aware of the great range of cheeses made on the

having declined throughout the 19th century and reaching an all-time low during World War 2. Over 200 different farm-made cheeses are made in Britain today and new producers are appearing on the scene all the time — often reviving and adapting recipes that are centuries old and using time-honoured methods. The vast majority of these cheeses are what are called specialist cheeses, which means they are made in the traditional way, more often than not with unpasteurised milk, but always with a real commitment to quality. Traditionally noted for its hard cows' milk cheeses, Britain can now boast a range of goats' and sheep's milk cheeses which are beginning to rival those available from Europe.

Although the growing demand for these cheeses means that an increasing number of specialist cheese shops are appearing around the country and many delicatessens are stocking a wider range of British cheeses, many are not made in sufficient quantities to be always widely available. Certainly you will have to go further afield than the local supermarket for most of the cheeses in this book, and some can only be obtained locally or by mail order.

Continent, but fewer may realise just how many are now made in Britain apart from Stilton and the eight territorials — Cheddar, Cheshire, Caerphilly, Derby, Double Gloucester, Lancashire, Red Leicester and Wensleydale.

During recent years the art of cheesemaking has been revived with a vengeance on British farms,

Making the Cheese

Rural History Centre
University of Reading

The History of Cheese

The domestication of animals began in India and the Middle East in around 5000BC and with migration this spread through Africa and into Europe, where the first cattle to be domesticated were the wild aurochs, a breed which became extinct in the early 17th century. With the domestication of cattle, sheep and goats came the beginnings of cheesemaking, as it was found that the curds of naturally souring milk could be drained of whey and eaten, albeit that they were very sharp and acid tasting.

However, the real beginnings of cheesemaking as we know it today came when it was discovered that the addition of rennin — an enzyme contained in the stomachs of unweaned mammals — to milk caused it to curdle without souring. Exactly how or when this discovery came about is again unclear, but one widely accepted theory is that nomads travelling across Central Asia carried their milk in pouches made from the stomachs of unweaned mammals and found that the milk curdled quickly yet remained sweet. Thus the magical properties of rennin, from which rennet is made, were discovered.

Cheese is certainly one of the oldest forms of prepared food in Britain, probably beginning with the

Ancient Britons, and within 300 years of the Roman invasion the practice of cheesemaking was well established and had become quite sophisticated.

After the fall of the Roman Empire, cheesemaking was taken up and developed in many religious dissolution of the monasteries, these cheesemaking skills were passed on to farmers in the region and local traditions took root.

By the 17th century cheeses came to be known by their regional names and the traditional cheeses we know

Rural History Centre
University of Reading

communities. The monks had the time, wealth and motivation (as there were many days in a year when meat-eating was renounced) to devote to cheesemaking and the craft was greatly influenced in Britain by monks from the Continent after the Norman Conquest. After the today became established, using almost exclusively cows' milk rather than the sheep's milk used before.

The 19th century, however, saw a marked change in the traditions of cheese-making. It began with widespread cattle disease in the 1860s which drastically reduced the availability of milk, and a shift of population from rural to urban areas, leaving fewer skilled cheesemakers working on the farms.

Mass production then began with the opening of the first cheese factory in Derby in 1870, to be rapidly followed by others throughout the country. Heat treatments were developed, mechanisation processes were introduced, and cheesemaking moved into the realms of commerce.

Traditional cheese-making nevertheless continued until World War 2 when all available milk for cheesemaking had to go to the factories making Cheddar, Cheshire, Leicester, Wensleydale and Dunlop. Stilton, Single and Double Gloucester, Caerphilly and Lancashire ceased to be made in the creameries, and on-farm cheesemaking ground to a halt. After the war only a fraction of on-farm cheesemakers resumed production and by the early 1950s traditional British cheese was in a sorry state. It took another 30-odd years of set-backs, ill-conceived regulations and dedication by a minority before it could be said to be back on its feet.

Since the 1980s, however, helped

*Rural History Centre
University of Reading*

by the fact that the ban on the use of unpasteurised milk was lifted, there has been a triumphant renaissance of traditionally made cheeses and the supply and demand for them is going from strength to strength.

A selection of composite cheeses.
Colin Peacock

Types of Cheese

Britain is traditionally known for its hard, mature cheeses made from cows' milk, but in fact an enormous number of different cheeses of all types are made in Britain today. Generally speaking, cheeses are described either as fresh, soft, semi-soft, semi-hard, hard or blue, but some are difficult to categorise and semi-soft and semi-hard in particular tend to merge.

Fresh Cheeses

These are unripened cheeses which have no rind and are of a mild, lactic flavour and a moist texture. Some are lightly pressed or hand moulded. They should be eaten immediately. Cream Cheese, Cottage Cheese, Curd Cheese, Fromage Frais and Quark are all fresh cheeses.

Soft Cheeses

High in moisture (and therefore usually low in fat), soft cheeses are traditionally associated with France — Brie and Camembert, for example — but more and more soft cheeses are being produced in Britain now.

Grazing sheep seen close to the River Tweed in Peebles-shire.
I. D. Washington/Nature Photographers Ltd

A dairy show. *J. P. Shelden*

character and texture. Either unpressed or lightly pressed, most can either be eaten young, when they have a light, fresh flavour and an open texture, or when ripened when the taste becomes stronger and the texture more springy.

Hard Cheeses

Very hard, dense cheeses which, due to their low moisture content, keep well. Ripening usually takes place over a much longer period of time than other types of cheese. They often have thick rinds, which may be waxed, oiled or bandaged.

Semi-soft Cheeses

Firmer than soft cheeses but moist and often springy or crumbly.

Semi-hard Cheese

The cheeses that fall into this category are very diverse in terms of

Blue Cheeses

These are cheeses veined with blue. At one time many cheeses acquired blue veining naturally due to a particular mould entering the cheese through tiny cracks and spreading through the curds. Called penicillium roquefortii because it occurs naturally in the famous caves in France where Roquefort is stored, among other places, it (or penicillium glaucum) is now added to the curds quite deliberately. Most blue cheeses are then pierced with wire needles to allow air in and the mould to develop along the 'tunnels'. All blue cheeses ripen from the centre outwards and most have a strong, piquant flavour and a pungent smell. They can be semi-hard, semi-soft or soft.

Other descriptions of cheese are as follows:

Jersey cows awaiting milking.
E. A. Janes/Nature Photographers Ltd

Toggenberg goat.
*S. C. Bisserot/Nature
Photographers Ltd*

Unpressed Cheeses
The curds are cut very little and left to drain naturally, without being pressed.

Pressed Uncooked Cheeses
The curds are pressed in varying degrees and ripened from between two and 18 months.

Pressed Cooked Cheeses
The curds are cooked before being pressed — heavily — and the cheese is matured for many months, even years.

Bloomy Rind Cheeses
Soft creamy cheeses with white fuzzy surface moulds. Unpasteurised milk produces natural, off-white mould, while cheeses made from pasteurised milk are sprayed with artificial snow-white mould. Ripening occurs from the outside in, usually taking no longer than two months. The rind is edible.

Washed Rind Cheeses
These soft or semi-soft cheeses have natural rinds which are rinsed (sometimes soaked) in brine, alcohol or oil to add flavour. Rich, vivid colours are imparted to the rind which has no mould growth but the sticky surface attracts a bacteria which assists ripening. These are the smelliest of cheeses, although often the interior is surprisingly mild in taste. The rind is not normally eaten.

Dry Natural Rind Cheeses
These cheeses come in all sorts of interesting shapes and sizes. They ripen from the inside out, and from the outside in — ideally at the same pace so an even texture results. The rind forms as the curds at the edge of the cheese dry out; they can be bandaged to make them coarse and textured, or oiled so they become smooth and shiny. These rinds are not, as a rule, eaten.

Artificial Rind Cheeses
These are coverings, such as wax, which are added by the cheesemaker.

Processed Cheeses
Cheeses combined with emulsifying salts, butter, mild powders and other additives. Sold pre-wrapped. Not to be recommended by anyone who takes cheese seriously, but they have their uses as a food source and keep well.

Composite Cheeses
These are made up of more than one basic cheese and are nearly always

creamery-made. Varieties tend to come and go quite quickly.

Cow, Sheep and Goat Cheeses

In Britain, all creamery-made cheese is made from cows' milk. As far as traditional, farm-made cheese is concerned, however, an increasing number of cheeses are now being made from ewes' and goats' milk. In general, cows' milk is used to make hard cheeses, whereas soft and semi-soft cheeses tend to be made from the milk of goats or ewes, although this is by no means always the case.

Goats' milk, naturally homogenised and high in fat and alkaline rather than acid, can impart a very distinctive flavour to the cheese. People who are allergic to cows' milk can often tolerate goats' milk, possibly because it does not contain many of the pathogens present in cows' milk. It is also easier to digest than cows' milk as the fat particles are smaller.

Rich without having a pronounced flavour, ewes' milk, like goats', is easily digested. Ewes' milk has the highest level of all of protein and vitamins and is higher in solids than cows' milk.

For easy reference, the cheeses described in this book are grouped here into cows', sheep's and goats' milk cheeses.

Cows' Milk Cheeses

Beamish
Bexton
Blue Cheshire
Blue Wensleydale
Bonchester
Botton
Caboc
Caerphilly
Caws Cenarth
Celtic Promise
Cheddar
Cheshire
Cloisters
Coquetdale
Cornish Yarg, Pepper, Herb and Garlic
Cotherstone
Coverdale
Crannog
Crofton (with goats' milk)
Cumberland Farmhouse
Curworthy
Derby
Devon Blue
Devon Garland
Devon Oke
Dorset Blue Vinney
Double Berkeley
Double Gloucester
Double Worcester
Dunlop
Dunsyre Blue
Elgar
Finn
Flower Marie
Fountains Gold
Galic
Gospel Green
Gowrie
Gruth Dhu
Hereford Hop
Highland Crowdie
Hramsa
Isle of Mull
Jersey Blue
Jervaulx
Kelsae
Lancashire
Little Derby
Llanboidy
Llangloffan
Newbury

Northumberland
Old Sussex
Old Worcester White
Orkney
Pencarreg
Pencarreg Blue
Red Cheshire
Red Leicester
Ribblesdale
Sage Derby
St Illtyd
Severn Sisters
Sharpham
Shropshire Blue
Single Gloucester
Somerset Blue
Somerset Brie
Staffordshire Organic
Stichill
Stilton
Stinking Bishop
Swaledale Cheese
Teifi
Teviotdale
Tobermory
Tornegus
Torville
Tynedale Spa
Tyn Grug
Waterloo
Wealden Round
Wedmore
Wellington
Wensleydale
Wigmore
Worcestershire Gold
Worcestershire Sauce
Yorvik

Goats' Milk Cheeses

Allerdale
Ashdale
Ash Pyramid
Baby Brendon
Ballindalloch
Basing
Blackdown
Bonnet
Brendon Blue
Burndell
Capricorn
Caprini
Cerney
Chabis
Chancton
Crofton (with cows' milk)
Elsdon
Galloway Goats
Gedi cheeses
Gobhar
Golden Cross
Harbourne Blue
Hazlewood
Innes cheeses
Irthingspa
Loddiswell Banon
Mendip
Merlin cheeses
Nanny's Cheddar
Pant-ysgawn
Perroche
Pyramid
Ragstone
Ribblesdale
Rosary Plain
St George
Sleight

Thistledown
Ticklemore Goat
Tymsboro'
Vulscombe

Sheep's Milk Cheeses

Acorn
Beenleigh Blue
Bewcastle
Bexton Ewes Milk in Oil
Birling
Carolina
Cecelia
Coleford Blue
Crowlink
Cwm Tawe
Duddleswell
Dunwick
Emlett
Herriot Farmhouse
Heydale cheeses
Lanark Blue
Leafield
Little Rydings
Malvern
Nepicar
Nuns of Caen
Olde York
Quantock Blue
Redesdale
Ribblesdale
Skirrid
Spenwood
Sussex Slipcote
Swaledale Ewes
Swinzie
Tala
Tyning
Walda
Yorkshire Blue
Yorkshire Lowlands
Farmhouse Cheese

How Cheese is Made

Making cheese in the traditional manner is a very individual and infinitely variable process, but, whatever the end product, the basic principles are the same. All creamery-made cheese produced in Britain is made from pasteurised cows' milk which ensures a uniform and consistent product. Unpasteurised milk, on the other hand, varies considerably according to the factors given below and batches of cheese from the same farm can differ quite noticeably — which of course is part of the charm. The use of goats' and ewes' milk has increased considerably in recent years.

A variety of items used in cheese-making in the early 20th century. *Rural History Centre University of Reading*

Longford cheese factory.
J. P. Shelden

Ingredients

The raw ingredient used to make cheese is milk and as this can vary tremendously (in its untreated state) it is the key to the huge range of flavours and consistencies of which cheese can boast.

One of the chief factors, of course, is whether the milk has come from a cow, a sheep or a goat (see page 12), but other influences affecting the milk include the breed of animal, the age of the animal, the time of year, the fodder the animal has been given, the type of grazing and the nature of the soil, whether or not artificial fertilizers have been used on the pasture, the stage of lactation the animal has reached, the time of milking (morning or evening) and even the weather on the day of milking.

Coagulation

The first stage of cheesemaking is to coagulate the milk, ie to extract the water from the milk (the whey) leaving the milk solids (the curds) behind. Left to its own devices, milk will sour and coagulate naturally, but this is an unpredictable business and cheesemakers nowadays add a 'starter' of lactic-acid forming bacteria to the milk which hastens and controls the natural souring process. Some cheeses, known as lactic-curd or acid-curd cheeses, are coagulated entirely by lactic acid, but most require the addition of rennet when acidity levels are right. This causes a reaction in the milk that separates the curds from the whey — coagulation.

Cutting and Treating the Curds

The next stage is to cut and treat the curds. Cutting releases more whey, so how this is done and to what extent determines the moisture content and thus the texture of the finished cheese. The curds of softer cheeses, for example, are not cut as much as those of hard cheeses and may be drained naturally rather than being pressed. The curds may also be heated (a

Whey being drained from the curds of Lancashire Cheese.
Farmhouse Cheesemakers Ltd

process known as scalding), causing them to become more compact and release yet more whey.

It is at this stage of production that any flavourings are added to the curds.

Moulding and Pressing

The next stage is to transfer the curds into moulds, which are perforated to allow further drainage of the whey. The curds are then either left alone to become firm naturally or are pressed in varying degrees. Moulds can be made of almost anything and come in

Salting the curds.
Farmhouse Cheesemakers Ltd

Placing a cloth around a cylindrical Cheddar
Farmhouse Cheesemakers Ltd

Ripening

Ripening is the final stage of cheesemaking during which the cheese matures, and the length of time this takes varies between types of cheese. For example, fresh cheeses are not ripened at all and a mature Cheddar can be ripened for two years or more.

Temperature and humidity in the cheese store has to be carefully controlled throughout the ripening period, and cheesemakers have to be extremely vigilant, constantly checking colour, texture and smell. Cheeses also have to be regularly turned to ensure uniform maturity, and to prevent one end drying out and the other becoming soggy.

a vast array of shapes and sizes. Some cheeses are still transferred into a cheesecloth and moulded by hand.

Finishing

Cheeses can then be 'finished' in a variety of ways, including bandaging or waxing, soaking in brine, spraying with artificial mould, coating in herbs or ashes or covering with cloth or plastic.

It is during ripening that cheeses acquire their individual characteristics and tastes: veining begins in blue cheeses, moulds form on the outside and so on. As a general rule, particularly for hard cheeses, the longer a cheese is matured, the stronger becomes its flavour.

Buying, Keeping and Serving Cheese

Buying

Whatever cheese you are buying, the criterion should be the same — quality.

If possible, go to a reputable cheesemonger who keeps his cheeses well and can offer advice if need be. At a shop like this, too, you should always be able to sample a particular cheese before buying. If possible, always buy from a whole cheese rather than settling for pre-cut pieces — whatever the protestations that it was 'cut this morning'.

Beware of sweaty cheese and hard or cracked surfaces; any hint of ammonia in the aroma indicates the cheese is past its best. Soft cheeses should be springy to the touch and of an even consistency throughout; they should not be too runny or have a chalky, solid centre.

Keeping

Cheese is not the easiest of foods to keep and a certain amount of care is required if it is to be enjoyed at its best. In general, it is best to buy only as much cheese as is likely to be consumed within a few days.

For a start, cheese does not like extremes of temperature (the optimum is just over 10°C/50°F) which is unfortunate as most householders have to choose between a warm kitchen cupboard or the fridge — neither of which is ideal. If you are a cheese connoisseur the very best places to store cheese are cellars and larders, but in the absence of these old-fashioned luxuries, garages or outhouses kitted out with a well-ventilated box or cupboard are good substitutes.

In the event of cheese having to be kept in a fridge, store in the warmest part — the door or the vegetable compartment — and wrap well in foil then place inside a plastic box. When not refrigerated, however, cheese must be allowed to breathe, so wrap in a clean tea towel, foil, waxed or greaseproof paper. Cut surfaces of cheese should be tightly covered, and those of soft cheeses

CHEESEMONGER

A Victorian cheesemonger.
Rural History Centre University of Reading

should be prevented from 'running away' by placing against a firm surface.

The length of time cheese can be stored varies tremendously, according to its moisture content. Fresh cheeses, which have a high moisture content, should be eaten within a day or two of purchase. Semi-hard and hard cheeses can be kept reasonably well in the right conditions, but soft cheeses do not fare well after a few days.

Cheeses that have been bought sealed in plastic may sweat, so remove, dry, and rewrap in waxed paper, greaseproof paper or foil.

Unopened vacuum-packed cheeses will keep for several weeks or even months if stored in a cold place.

Whole cheeses which have not yet been cut should be turned every week or so to prevent one end becoming too dry and the other too moist. When ready to cut, uncover only as much of the cheese as necessary and cut in rings. Seal the cut surface and wrap immediately.

Freezing is not recommended for good table cheeses, but it is possible with some. The disadvantages are that hard cheeses tend to crumble when thawed, making them suitable only for cooking (although this can be offset to some degree by

Inside a Stilton cheese maturing room. *Osborne Publicity*

Cheese served with fruits and nuts. *National Dairy Council*

defrosting in the fridge), and soft cheeses tend to lose their flavour. Fresh cheeses are probably best suited to freezing.

Serving

It goes without saying that cheese should be bought as near to the time it is required so it is in peak condition when served. It is also important to remove it from the fridge at least one to two hours before serving so it has time to reach room temperature. Do not uncover until the last minute so it can acclimatise gradually and there is no danger of it drying out.

When composing a cheeseboard it is better to go for a few good, carefully selected cheeses rather than a host chosen at random 'to give plenty of choice'.

As well as taking into account what type of food has previously been served — rich, spicy etc — and the accompanying wines, the criteria for composing a cheeseboard should be to offer a balance of taste, texture and colour. Choosing one cheese from four or five 'types' (see page 9) is a good starting point, and after that it is down to experience, commonsense and a good cheesemonger!

Do give guests as much information about the cheeses you are serving as you can, and as ideally they should be eaten in ascending order of strength to be fully appreciated, point this out, too. Provide at least two cheese-knives — one for mild, one for strong cheeses.

Serve fresh, plain biscuits, crackers or oatcakes; cheesy-flavoured biscuits are best avoided. Good, fresh bread, rye bread or fruit bread are other options. Some people like butter with their cheese, some don't, but unsalted butter is probably preferable as it interferes less with the flavour of the cheeses. Ignore any affectations claiming that it is not the done thing to eat butter with cheese.

Other accompaniments are a matter of choice: apples, grapes, celery, radishes and nuts — in moderation — can all enhance the appearance of a cheeseboard.

The French habit of serving cheese before the pudding has much to recommend it if you are planning to serve a dessert wine.

Cooking with Cheese

Baked potato with cheese and chives. *Food Features*

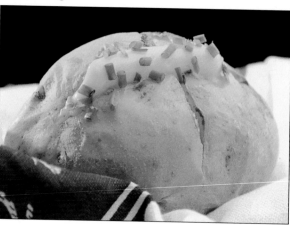

Hard Cheeses

These cook better if grated first. The stronger the cheese, the less you will need, and the harder it is the better it will blend with other ingredients.

Cheese is a tremendously useful and versatile cooking ingredient, but it needs treating with just as much respect when used in cooked dishes as it does when eaten on its own. It is also a mistake to think that second-rate cheese will do.

The first and most important thing to remember when cooking cheese is not to overcook it — doing so will make it hard and stringy because the protein in cheese separates from the fat and water over 55.5°C (150°F).

A second general rule is to add the cheese to the other ingredients at the last possible moment. This applies particularly to sauces; remember that cheese only has to be melted to impart its flavour.

Some cheeses are more suitable for cooking than others, with different types lending themselves to different uses.

Hard cheeses are particularly suitable for crispy toppings, especially when mixed with breadcrumbs or other starchy foods. Cheddar is the most widely used and versatile hard cooking cheese, but almost any hard cheese can be grated successfully. Cheshire is another excellent all-round hard cooking cheese.

Double Gloucester, Red Leicester and Scottish Cheddar impart their colour to dishes; Cheshire and Lancashire are good for soups; Lancashire and Red Leicester are excellent for toasting.

Soft Cheeses

As they have a higher water or fat content than hard cheeses, soft cheeses can be satisfactorily blended with similar liquids such as cream or vinaigrette to make interesting dips and sauces.

Many soft cheeses are also good for mashing as a filling for baked potatoes, tomatoes or peppers, or crumbling over green vegetables just prior to serving.

Soft cheeses flavoured with herbs can be spread on grilled meat or fish.

Blue Cheeses
These can be crumbled and added to salads, or used in salad dressings. They melt well in sauces and retain their flavour well when cooked; they

A cheese and vegetable pie.
Food Features.

are good in soups and pâtés, or grilled with meat. Grate any blue cheese straight from the fridge.

Bloomy Rind Cheeses
These do not melt well, but they can be crumbled, deep-fried or grilled successfully.

Fresh Cheeses
Cottage, curd and cream cheeses are good for sweet dishes. They melt easily, but curdle quickly.

Traditional Regional Cheese Dishes
Cheese dishes, like any others, have their place in traditional regional cooking in Britain. The following recipes are intended to be just a taster.

Glamorgan Sausages
These contain no meat. George Borrow, writing in Wild Wales (1862) considered these sausages 'Not a whit inferior to those of Epping' which was praise indeed, because Epping was famous for its skinless pork sausages. According to David Mabey, the original cheese used for making this delicacy was Glamorgan, which was made from the milk of a breed of white cow called Gwent.

As with all traditional dishes, the recommended proportions of ingredients varies from recipe to recipe. Here is one:

Mix 4oz of white breadcrumbs with 4oz of grated Caerphilly cheese.

Stir in $1/2$ tbsp finely chopped leek or spring onion, $1/2$ tsp dry mustard powder and $1/2$ tsp thyme, salt and freshly ground black pepper. Bind the mixture with the yolk of 1 egg (reserve the white). If the mixture is too dry, add a little water; if too wet, breadcrumbs.

Form sausage shapes with the mixture, dip first in the beaten egg white, then in some extra breadcrumbs, and fry until golden brown.

Yorkshire Curd Cheesecakes

These are based on the simple fresh curd tarts which became popular in medieval times. Traditionally they were baked at Melton Mowbray in Leicestershire for the Whitsuntide Feast, and various highdays and holidays at other villages in the region. It was in Yorkshire, home of the high tea, where they became most famous.

Heat oven to 425°F/220°C/mark 7
Line one 8in flan case or 24 small patty-pans with 8oz shortcrust pastry.
Cream together 4oz butter, 2-3oz castor sugar and 8oz curd cheese.
Add 3oz currants, a heaped tsp of grated lemon rind and 1tbsp of wholemeal breadcrumbs. Stir in 2 beaten eggs.
Fill the pastry cases with the mixture, then sprinkle generously with freshly grated nutmeg.
Bake for 20-30min until filling is set and the pastry crisp.

Cheese Roasted and Toasted

In 1612 Thomas Cogan wrote disapprovingly that 'roasted cheese is more meet to bait a trap, than to be received into the body'.

There are many regional variations on this, the most basic way of cooking cheese. Here is one old recipe:

Gloucester Cheese and Ale

Remove the rind from some Double or Single Gloucester cheese, then shave thin pieces into an oven-proof dish, to cover the bottom with a generous layer.
Spread English mustard over the cheese, then pour over enough strong ale to cover.
Cook in a hot oven until the cheese is melted. Meanwhile, make some thick pieces of wholemeal toast, moisten them with a sprinkling of ale, then pour or spoon on the cheese mixture.
Serve very hot with a mug of frothing ale and some English pickles.

Welsh Rabbit (Rare-bit)

There are many variations of this. Hannah Glasse gives one in her cookery book of 1747. Jane Grigson suggests using Lancashire, Cheddar or Double Gloucester. Mrs Beeton suggests Cheshire or Gloucester. If using Cheddar, it should be a good-flavoured variety.
Put a large knob of butter in a small heavy saucepan and melt

over a low heat.

Stir in twice as much ale, a twist of freshly ground black pepper and 1tsp of English mustard (wholegrain is good).

When the mixture starts to simmer, gently stir in enough grated cheese to make a thick cream. Do not let the mixture boil.

Adjust seasoning.

Place two slices of thick wholemeal toast on a heat-proof dish, pour over the cheese mixture and brown under the grill.

Serve very hot, garnished with sliced tomatoes and parsley, and with a glass of good beer.

Scotch Rabbit

According to Hannah Glasse, this has no ale and the cheese is toasted separately, then added to the toasted bread.

English Rabbit

This combines cheese with red wine.

Theodora Fitzgibbon gives an old Cheshire recipe for toasted cheese: the Cheshire cheese is grated and combined with breadcrumbs, egg yolks and a little milk, spread on bread which has been toasted on one side only, then placed in an oven, or under a grill, to cook.

According to Joan Poulson, to make a Yorkshire Rabbit, the melted cheese is topped with a fat slice of bacon and an egg — Yorkshire is, of course, famous for its bacon.

Potted Cheeses

These were very popular in the 18th and 19th centuries and there are many variations: Hannah Glasse combines 3lb of Cheshire cheese with 1/2lb of butter and 1/4 pint of rich Canary wine. Florence White quotes a 1930s recipe which recommends North Wiltshire as the best, combined with butter, sherry and ground mace.

Stilton is good with port, and home-made potted Stilton with port makes a nice Christmas gift. Potted cheeses were preserved by pouring clarified butter over the top to exclude air.

Apple Pie and Cheese

'An apple pie without some cheese
Is like a kiss without a squeeze.'

You can put the wisdom of this old Lancashire saying into practice by sprinkling grated Lancashire cheese over the raw apple filling of a pie before putting the pastry lid on and cooking the pie.

A-Z

of British
Cheeses

For a quick-reference list of cows', sheep's or goats' cheese, see page 12

Acorn

Produced on a farm in Dyfed, this full-fat hard cheese is made with no additives or preservatives other than pure salt. Resembling traditional Wensleydale, it is clean tasting, dry and full flavoured; its pale colour acquires a bluish tinge after cutting. Autumn batches are best.

Little Acorn Products, Bethania, Dyfed, Wales. Unpasteurised sheep's milk. Vegetarian rennet. 5-5.5lb truckles.

Acorn cheese. *Supplied by Paxton & Whitfield; Food Features*

Allerdale

A full-fat, semi-hard, moist cheese with a sweetish flavour and a smooth texture. Also available smoked. Coated in natural wax. Best after six weeks of maturing, although also available at two to three weeks of age.

Thornby Moor Dairy, Wigton, Cumbria. Unpasteurised goats' milk. Vegetarian rennet. 1lb, 2lb and 5lb truckles.

Cumberland Farmhouse cheese.
Supplied by Paxton & Whitfield; Food Features

Appleby's Double Gloucester
see Double Gloucester

Appleby's Hawkstone Cheshire
see Cheshire

Ashdale

A hard, mild cheese that keeps for at least three months without acquiring a goaty taste. It comes coated in yellow wax.

Town Head Farm, Askwith, near Otley, North Yorkshire. Unpasteurised goats' milk. Vegetarian rennet. 3-4lb and 10oz individuals.

Ash Pyramid

A smooth, soft cheese made in the shape of a dumpy pyramid and coated with ash. Light-textured and tangy.

Sleight Farm, Timsbury, Avon. Unpasteurised goats' milk. Vegetarian rennet. 7oz individuals.

Baby Brendon

A small, soft cheese usually sold at between four and eight weeks old. It can then be kept for up to another eight weeks in the fridge. Made from the milk of the same flocks used to produce Brendon Blue.

Exmoor Blue Cheeses, Willett Farm Dairy, Lydeard St Lawrence, Somerset. Unpasteurised goats' milk. Vegetarian rennet. 10-17oz.

Ballindalloch

A smooth-textured full-fat hard cheese with a natural rind. Matured for at least two months for anything up to a year, it has a good flavour without being goaty.

Highland Goat Products, Ballindalloch, Banffshire, Scotland. Unpasteurised goats' milk. Vegetarian rennet. 4-5lb truckles.

Ballindalloch cheese. *Supplied by Jeroboam's; Food Features*

27

Basing

Full-fat, lightly pressed, moist, crumbly, mild, creamy flavoured cheese which becomes even creamier with age. A smoked version is also available.

Lower Basing Farm, Cowden, Kent. Unpasteurised goats' milk. Vegetarian rennet. 3lb truckles, 9lb rounds and vacuum-packed wedges.

Beamish

This hard cheese is made at the dairy of the Beamish Open Air Museum by the Swaledale Cheese Co and sold direct to visitors. Mild with a lemony freshness, it is a cloth-bound hard cheese which is matured for six weeks.

Home Farm, Beamish, Co Durham. Pasteurised cows' milk. Vegetarian rennet if required. 1.6lb, and larger sizes on request.

Beenleigh Blue

Made from the milk of Dorset/Friesland-cross ewes that graze on the banks of the River Dart. They are milked between March and July only, so seasonal availability. This strongly flavoured, semi-hard moist cheese with light, blue-green veining becomes creamier with age. It is matured for seven months underground and has a natural rind. It comes wrapped in greaseproof paper.

Ticklemore Cheese, Totnes, Devon. Pasteurised sheep's milk. 6lb wheels.

Belstone see Curworthy

Bewcastle

Smooth, lightly pressed cheese with a pure lactic flavour. Available plain, with garlic, or oak smoked. It keeps very well and comes waxed, or with a rind.

Thornby Moor Dairy, Wigton, Cumbria. Unpasteurised sheep's milk. Vegetarian rennet. 1-5lb cylindricals and 4lb truckles.

Bexton

A soft cheese with a pale-orange washed rind. A smoked version — Bexton Smoked — is also available.

Bexton Cheese, The Dairy, Knutsford, Cheshire. Pasteurised cows' milk. Vegetarian rennet. 8oz rounds.

Birling

This is a distinctive, supple cheese not unlike a White Stilton in taste. During the summer the dairy is open to visitors.

Seven Sisters Sheep Centre, East Dean, East Sussex. Pasteurised sheep's milk. Vegetarian rennet. 2lb.

Blackdown

A full-fat, soft cheese with a clean, delicate flavour.

Blackdown Farm, Loddiswell, Devon. Unpasteurised goats' milk. Vegetarian rennet. 8oz, 1lb, 2lb and 6lb rounds.

Blue Cheshire see Cheshire

Blue Vinney see Dorset Blue Vinney

Blue Wensleydale see
Wensleydale

Bonchester
Made from the milk of grass-fed
Jersey cows between March and
December on the borders of
Scotland, at Bonchester Bridge, so
only seasonally available. When ripe,
this mould-ripened soft full-fat
cheese has a thick, buttery texture
and a sweetish, well-defined flavour.
May be eaten when young and mild,
or matured for up to five weeks,
when it is stronger, softer and a
deeper yellow.
*Easter Weens, Bonchester Bridge,
Hawick, Scotland. Unpasteurised
cows' milk. Vegetarian/non
vegetarian rennet.*

Bonnet
Mild, white, moist, crumbly pressed
cheese not unlike Wensleydale. It

Bonchester cheese. *Supplied by
Neal's Yard Dairy; Food Features*

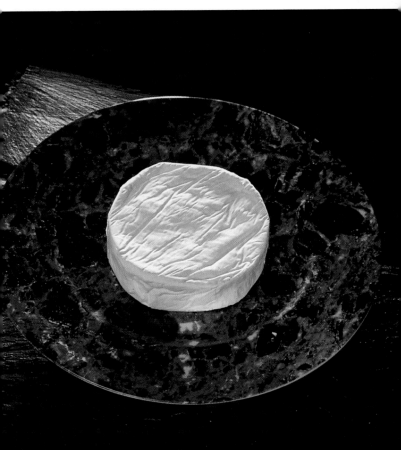

derives its name from the local cottage industry of bonnet-making for the Highland armies.
Dunlop Dairy Products, Stewarton, Scotland. Pasteurised goats' milk. Vacuum-packed.

Botton

Organically-made hard cheese resembling Cheddar, based on a traditional Dales recipe. Can be matured for up to a year, during which time it develops a rich, smoky flavour.
Botton Creamery, Danby, North Yorkshire. Unpasteurised cows' milk. Vegetarian rennet. 15.5lb.

Brendon Blue

A full-fat, unpressed blue cheese that is matured for three to four months. It is made from the milk of three pedigree flocks — British Saanen, British Alpine and British Toggenberg. The initial white colour of the cheese acquires a brownish tinge with age, and it has a natural crust resembling that of Stilton.
Exmoor Blue Cheeses, Willett Farm Dairy, Lydeard St Lawrence, Somerset. Unpasteurised goats' milk. Vegetarian rennet. 5.5lb truckles.

Burndell

A full-fat pressed cheese which is matured for at least two months, giving it a clean, creamy, non-goaty flavour. Coated in yellow wax.
Malthouse Cottage Farm, Ashington, West Sussex. Pasteurised goats' milk. Vegetarian rennet. 3lb wheels.

Caboc

Traditionally said to have been first made by the daughter of a Scottish chieftain from the Western Isles in the 16th century, this rich, creamy fresh cheese is rolled in toasted pinhead oatmeal and has a mild, nutty flavour. It should be eaten when very new.
Highland Fine Cheeses Ltd, Tain, Scotland. Pasteurised cows' milk. Unrenneted.

Caerphilly

This mild, white, moist, crumbly cheese with a slightly sour, salty flavour takes its name from the Welsh town in Mid-Glamorgan. First made on farms twice daily in the early 19th century from the milk of the Hereford cows in the area, it quickly became a favourite with miners who took it underground in cake-like wedges to eat at lunchtime; it did not dry out and its saltiness helped replenish salt lost while working.

One of Caerphilly's great advantages was its quick ripening properties — it is ready for sale within two weeks of milking — and the cheesemakers on the other side of the Bristol Channel cashed in on this fact by producing Caerphilly while their Cheddars were maturing.

During World War 2 production of Caerphilly was halted as a result of milk rationing and since its recommencement in the early 1950s it has been largely factory made. Caerphilly is not to everyone's taste when cooked.
Pasteurised cows' milk. Creamery-made cheese widely available.

Caerphilly. *National Dairy Council*

Farmhouse Caerphilly see Caws Cenarth

Glynhynod Caerphilly

Glynhynod Organic Farmers, Llandysul, Dyfed, Wales. Unpasteurised cows' milk. Vegetarian rennet.

See Caws Cenarth Caerfilli

Capricorn

One herd of British Saanen goats in Somerset produces the milk for this soft, mould-ripened cheese that was first made in the early 1980s. Mildly flavoured and very smooth, it ripens from the outside and gets only slightly stronger as it does so. It should be eaten immediately once cut.

Capricorn cheese. *Supplied by Paxton & Whitfield; Food Features*

Lubborn Cheese Ltd, Crewkerne, Somerset. Pasteurised goats' milk. Vegetarian rennet. 2lb bricks, 3.5oz cylindrical cheeses.

Caprini

Full-fat slices or balls of soft cheese marinated in seven varieties of herbs and oil and sold bottled.

Nut Knowle Farm, Woodmancote, *West Sussex. Pasteurised goats' milk. Vegetarian rennet.*

Carolina

Now produced on a farm in Kent to a 12th-century recipe, Carolina takes its name from the pastures in Somerset where it was first made. A dark coloured, greyish-brown natural rind covers this strongly flavoured, firm-textured cheese which has a lemony tang to it. After being individually pressed, the larger cheeses are matured for two months, the smaller for six weeks.

British Sheep Dairy Products, Wrotham Heath, Kent. Unpasteurised/pasteurised sheep's milk. Vegetarian rennet. 16-24oz rounds, 4.5-6lb

Caws Cenarth

A range of creamy-textured, moist, firm Caerphilly cheeses in a smooth, waxed rind. As well as young Caerphilly which is available oak-smoked or with fresh herbs, more mature cheeses are made with flavourings such as pears with pineapple liqueur, fresh peppers and white wine and sun-dried tomatoes with white wine.

Caws Cenarth, Pontesili, Dyfed, Wales. Unpasteurised cows' milk. Vegetarian rennet. 1lb, 2lb and 10lb rounds.

Cecilia

A hard cheese matured in oak barrels placed on Kentish hops — which impart a subtle flavour to the cheese. Firm and moist-textured with a natural yellowish-grey rind.

British Sheep Dairy Products, Wrotham Heath, Kent. Unpasteurised/pasteurised sheep's milk. Vegetarian rennet. 16-24oz rounds, 4.5-6lb.

Celtic Promise

James Aldridge takes Glynhynod Organic Farmers' 1lb Caerphilly minis and matures them in cider to produce a semi-soft, rind-washed cheese.

James Aldridge, Rooks Farm, near Godstone, Surrey. Unpasteurised cows' milk cheese. Vegetarian rennet. 1lb minis.

Cerney cheeses

Five soft goat cheeses named after the village in which they are made.

Cerney — a squat, pyramid-shaped 8oz cheese coated with a dark grey blend of oak ash and sea salt. Semi-hard, mild and fresh tasting.

Celtic Promise.
Supplied by Paxton & Whitfield; Food Features

Cerney Smoked — a full-fat, round, 8oz smoked cheese.

Cerney Pepper — a mild, small, round fresh cheese flavoured with coarse ground pepper.

Cerney Orange — a 3oz cheese flavoured with orange and Grand Marnier and coated with toasted almonds.

Cerney Starter — a soft, 2oz cheese ideal for grilling.
Cerney Cheese, North Cerney, near Cirencester, Gloucestershire. Unpasteurised goats' milk. Vegetarian rennet.

Chabis

Small, soft, creamy individual cheeses coated in white mould when mature. *Greenacres Farm, near Lewes, East Sussex. Unpasteurised goats' milk. Vegetarian rennet.*

Chancton

Made from the milk of goats mostly fed organically and grazed on the South Downs, this is a soft creamy cutting cheese with a mould-ripened crust. Mild and fairly firm when

Chabis cheese. *Supplied by Neal's Yard Dairy; Food Features*

young, it softens and acquires a well-defined flavour as it matures.

Malthouse Cottage Farm, Ashington, West Sussex. Pasteurised goats' milk. Vegetarian rennet. 2lb discs.

Cheddar

This is without doubt Britain's most famous and widely used all-purpose cheese; it has also suffered greatly as a result of extensive mechanisation processes and being made into rindless blocks instead of traditional cylindricals. There are dozens of Cheddars on the market, most of which are creamery-made in blocks, but there are also several farmhouse cheeses available. These have been cut from a whole cheese, have been matured traditionally for much longer and are infinitely superior in terms of flavour. Having tasted traditionally matured Cheddar, nothing else will do.

Cheddar-making began in the 16th century in the Mendip Hills around Cheddar Gorge in Somerset and quickly became a firm favourite

Cheddar cheese. *Supplied by Neal's Yard Dairy; Food Features*

with all walks of society. Such was its popularity that travellers to other countries took the recipe with them, and thus we have Canadian Cheddar, New Zealand Cheddar, etc.

Up until the mid-19th century the making of Cheddar was a very variable business, but in 1856 a man called Joseph Harding perfected and standardised the method of cheesemaking, thus earning himself the nickname 'father of Cheddar'.

Traditional English Cheddar

comes from Somerset, Dorset or Devon. Colour can range from almost white through varying shades of yellow to deep orange, depending on the amount of annatto used, but the texture should always be consistently close and firm and not crumbly when cut. This texture is achieved by cheddaring, the process which distinguishes Cheddar from other hard cheeses. The curds are cut into blocks then repeatedly stacked and turned — so that the maximum amount of whey can be drained off — until they become smooth and elastic — thus producing the very even and smooth texture required.

Cheddar is sold at various stages of maturity:

Mild Cheddar is mellow and slightly sweet — usually sold after three to five months.

Mature Cheddar, matured for at least nine months, has much more bite and a nutty flavour to it.

Farmhouse Cheddar is matured for a minimum of 12 months and consequently acquires a deeper, more individual flavour. It is packed in cylindrical moulds lined with a greased bandage which causes a hard rind to form.

Scottish Cheddar is usually redder in colour than English Cheddar due to the use of annatto. A mature, black-waxed Cheddar is also produced in Scotland.

Flavoured Cheddars include:

Admirals — port and Stilton layers

Albany — cumin seed

Applewood — smoked and sprinkled with paprika

Charnwood — paprika; lightly smoked

Cheviot — chives

Five Counties — Cheddar, Double Gloucester, Cheshire, Derby and Red Leicester in layers

Glenphilly — malt whisky

Ilchester — beer, spices and chives

Nutcracker — walnuts

Nutwood — cider, raisins and hazelnuts

Oakwood — smoked

Penmill — peppercorns

Rutland — beer, garlic and parsley

Somerton — garlic and herbs

Waldorf — apple, pineapple, hazelnuts and celery

Walton — Stilton and hazelnuts

Windsor Red — elderberry wine

Yeoman — sweet pickle

see Farmhouse Cheeses

Cheshire

Mentioned in Domesday, this is one of Britain's oldest cheeses, and it may be that Celtic tribes were making it before the Romans came. It

Cheshire. *National Dairy Council*

Appleby's Cheshire cheese. *Supplied by Neal's Yard Dairy; Food Features*

was first known to have been made near Chester on the banks of the River Dee.

Cheshire cheese has a fine, moist, crumbly texture with a characteristic salty tang that comes from the salty deposits of the Cheshire Plain where it is traditionally made. It does not keep well and should be eaten fresh. Most Cheshire cheese is factory-made now, but a few farms make it traditionally. From them it comes bound with cloths dipped in lard or waxed. In the past, Cheshire cheeses were much larger than they are today.

Red Cheshire is exactly the same as White Cheshire except that annatto has been added.

Blue Cheshire, made with unpasteurised milk, has a stronger taste than either Red or White Cheshire and is less heavily pressed. It is said that, very occasionally, a Cheshire cheese will turn blue of its own accord, but you may have to wait several hundred years for this to happen! Nowadays *penicillium roquefortii* is added. The paste is coloured orange with annatto and the cheese has a thick, rough natural crust.

Cheshire is a very useful cooking cheese, going particularly well with eggs.

see Farmhouse Cheeses

Cheshire, Shropshire and Clwyd. Pasteurised cows' milk. Creamery-made cheese widely available.

Appleby's Hawkstone Cheshire

A pinkish-orange hard-pressed cheese that has earned itself a wide reputation. Crumbly, moist and tangy, it is bound in calico. An oak-smoked variety, Appleby's Smoked Cheshire, is also available in 2.75lb cylindricals and 5.5lb wheels.

Appleby's of Hawkstone, near Whitchurch, Shropshire.Unpasteurised cows' milk. 2.75lb, 5lb, 18lb and 50lb cylindricals.

Cloisters

Based on a cheese made by the Cistercian monks who farmed this part of Gloucestershire in the 13th century where this cheese is now made — hence the name. A soft, peppery cheese with an orange (annatto-washed), edible rind.

Charles Martell & Son, Dymock, Gloucestershire. Pasteurised cows' milk. Vegetarian rennet. 4lb wheels.

Coleford Blue

A blue-veined, full-fat, unpressed, semi-hard cheese with a strong flavour and firm, dry consistency. It is matured for two months and has a wrinkled, greyish crust.

Exmoor Blue Cheeses, Willett Farm Dairy, Lydeard St Lawrence, Somerset. Unpasteurised sheep's milk. Vegetarian rennet. 4.5-5.5lb, vacuum packed smaller quantities.

Coquetdale

A semi-hard, medium-fat, slightly salty-flavoured cheese with a greyish mould. Nutty in flavour, it softens with age.

Redesdale Sheep Dairy, Otterburn, Northumberland. Pasteurised cows' milk. 4lb discs.

Cornish Herb and Garlic

Soft, full-fat spreading cheese flavoured with herbs and garlic and rolled in chopped parsley.

Lynher Valley Dairy, near Liskeard, Cornwall. Pasteurised cows' milk. Vegetarian rennet. 1lb and 2lb truckles, 0.5lb half-moons.

Cornish Pepper

Soft, full-fat cheese coated with cracked black pepper.

Lynher Valley Dairy, near Liskeard, Cornwall. Pasteurised cows' milk. Vegetarian rennet. 1lb and 2lb truckles, 100g boxed tubs.

Cornish Yarg

Yarg is Gray spelt backwards. The Grays first made this cheese about 12 years ago from an old recipe, now taken over by Lynher Valley Dairy, which is open to the public from spring to autumn. A full-fat semi-hard Caerphilly-type cheese wrapped in nettles which turn dark-greeny black. The cheese is crumbly and has a fresh lemony taste; it softens and develops more character with age, ripening from the outside in.

Lynher Valley Dairy, near Liskeard, Cornwall. Pasteurised cows' milk. Vegetarian rennet. 2lb and 6.5lb wheels.

Cornish Yarg cheese. *Supplied by Jeroboam's; Food Features*

Cotherstone

At one time a famous Dales cheese, Cotherstone (pronounced Cutherstone) has been revived on a farm near Barnard Castle. Mild, buttery and soft — almost waxy, it has a nutty, slightly sharp flavour, with a soft, pale yellow natural crust. Both white and blue-veined varieties are available.

Teesdale, Co Durham. Unpasteurisd cows' milk. 2lb and 5lb wheels.

Cottage Cheese

A generic name for a bland (almost tasteless), low-fat granular fresh cheese nowadays beloved of slimmers. It is actually a very old form of cheese, traditionally made by cottagers since medieval times as a way of using up the skimmed milk. Usually sold in tubs, and available with various flavourings — pineapple, ham, chives etc. It is made by draining the curds of skimmed cows' milk and coating them in thin cream.

Coverdale

Cylindrical and cloth-bound, this crumbly white cheese has a nutty flavour. It was traditionally made with sheep's milk by monks after the

Cotherstone cheese. *Supplied by Neal's Yard Dairy; Food Features*

Norman Conquest. A version made with chives is also available.
Fountains Dairy Products, Kirkby Malzeard, North Yorkshire. Pasteurised cows' milk. Vegetarian rennet.

Crannog
A full-fat, soft, organically produced cheese with a mild but rounded flavour. It is produced in individual rounds and coated with wax. Also available with mixed herbs.

Loch Arthur Creamery is part of the Loch Arthur Community, an active community in which men and women with handicaps can lead a satisfying life.
Loch Arthur Creamery, Beeswing, Dumfries, Scotland. Unpasteurised cows' milk. Vegetarian rennet. 10oz rounds.

Cream Cheese
Made on farms for centuries by allowing the cream to solidify naturally and draining off the whey through muslin. Rich, buttery and spreadable, cream cheese is made from either pasteurised single cream or double cream.

Crofton

A lightly pressed, full-fat creamy cheese with a natural grey rind. It has a distinctive tang.
Thornby Moor Dairy, Wigton, Cumbria. Mixture of unpasteurised cows' and goats' milk. Vegetarian rennet. 2lb and 5lb discs.

Crowdie see Highland Crowdie

Crowlink

White, fresh, tangy and crumbly, this cheese is not unlike Wensleydale. The dairy is open to visitors during the summer.
Seven Sisters Sheep Centre, East Dean, East Sussex. Pasteurised sheep's milk. Vegetarian rennet.

Cumberland Farmhouse

Smooth, mellow, creamy-textured full-fat hard cheese with a cloth or wax finish. Varieties also available with garlic, dill, fennel or sage, or oak-smoked.
Thornby Moor Dairy, Cumbria. Unpasteurised cows' milk. 10lb (cloth-bound), 1lb, 2lb and 5lb waxed truckles.

Curd Cheese

This is a generic name for acid-curd fresh cheese. It can be made from either cows', goats' or sheep's milk, usually pasteurised. It may be low, medium or full-fat, and is soft and mild. Sometimes called lactic-curd cheese. After the curds have separated from the whey they are drained, then blended with salt and skimmed milk powder.

Curworthy

A 17th-century recipe is used to make this full-fat, semi-hard cheese from the farm's own herd of Friesian cows. Slightly sweet with a buttery flavour, it has a natural grey rind, or can be black-waxed. The flavour deepens and mellows with age.

Belstone is Curworthy made with vegetarian rennet.

Meldon is the version flavoured with ale and whole grain mustard seeds.

Devon Oke is made in 10lb truckles and matured for six months.
Curworthy Farm, near Okehampton, Devon. Pasteurised/unpasteurised cows' milk. 1lb, 2.5lb and 5lb truckles.

Cwmtawe

Sheep grazed on the wild pastures of the Brecon Beacons produce the milk for this Welsh Pecorino — Pecorino being a generic name for Italian cheeses made from sheep's milk. This is a Sardinian-style Pecorino, semi-hard and crumbly with a rich creamy aftertaste. In Italy it is named 'the vegetarian bacon' because it is often fried with eggs instead of bacon.
Ty Gwyn Farm, Ystalyfera, West Glamorgan, Wales. Unpasteurised sheep's milk. Vegetarian rennet. 1lb, 4.5lb.

Derby

One of Derby's claims to fame is that it was the first cheese to be 'factory-

Curworthy cheese. *Supplied by Paxton & Whitfield; Food Features*

made'. In 1870, at Longford, in Derbyshire, a factory making the cheese opened in a converted warehouse. This paved the way for mass production of cheese and within half a dozen years another ten factories had sprung up in the same region.

Derby, close-textured, rindless and mild in flavour, is usually sold when four to six weeks old, but maturer versions, six months old, are sometimes available.

Sage Derby, with added sage soaked in chlorophyll to produce its striking green marbled effect, was originally made for consumption at

harvest time and Christmas as the sage was believed to be good for the digestion. Both varieties are mostly factory-made now.
Pasteurised cows' milk. Creamery-made cheese widely available.

Variations include:
Celebrity — flavoured with celery seeds

Cromwell — layered with Red Leicester

Five Counties — Cheddar, Double Gloucester, Cheshire, Derby and Red Leicester in layers

Devon Blue
Made by the makers of the well-known Beenleigh Blue, this unpressed, strongly flavoured salted blue cheese is matured for four months and sold foil-wrapped.
Ticklemore Cheese, Totnes, Devon. Unpasteurised cows' milk. 6lb.

Devon Garland
Having been off the market for a while, Devon Garland is again being made by Peverstone Cheese. This hand-made, mild flavoured flaky semi-hard cheese is made in a wheel from the milk of Jersey cows to a traditional recipe. It has a high butter content and a thin crust. Fresh mixed herbs form a layer in the centre.
Peverstone Cheese, Mutterton, Devon. Unpasteurised cows' milk. Vegetarian rennet. 8lb wheels.

Sage Derby. *National Dairy Council*

Devon Blue cheese. *Supplied by Paxton & Whitfield; Food Features*

Devon Oke see Curworthy

Dorset Blue Vinney

A hard, blue-vein cheese that disappeared from the market in the early 1980s having at one time been made on numerous farms throughout Dorset. It was made from the buttermilk left after buttermaking and, left to its own devices in various farm buildings rich in mould spores, quickly turned 'blue'. Vinney comes from the old English word for mould — 'vinew'. Much folklore surrounded this cheese, including the claim that it had to be made and ripened in the tack room of a stable to attract the necessary bacteria, or stand next to muddy, smelly boots.

Now made on one farm only, using skimmed milk in the traditional manner, this firm, low-fat, dry-textured cheese has a unique flavour — softer and more rounded than that of Stilton. (In the past, poor-quality Stiltons often masqueraded as Blue Vinney.)

A commercially made Blue Vinney is made in Leicestershire.
Dorset Blue Cheese Co, Woodbridge Farm, Stock Gaylard, Dorset. Unpasteurised cows' milk. Vegetarian rennet.

Double Berkeley

A distinctive looking full-fat cheese that used to be made by farmers in the Berkeley area — hence its name. Annatto colouring is used to produce a subtle marbled effect.

Charles Martell, Dymock, Gloucestershire. Pasteurised cows' milk. Vegetarian rennet. 2lb and 8lb wheels.

Double Gloucester

Both Double and Single Gloucester originated in the Vale of Gloucester and the Vale of Berkeley some 1,000 years ago, but it was not until the early 18th century that the cheeses became popular further afield.

Dorset Blue Vinney cheese. *Supplied by Jeroboam's; Food Features*

There are two schools of thought as to how the names Single Gloucester and Double Gloucester came about. One claims that the name Double Gloucester stems from the fact that originally the cheese was made from both morning and evening milkings, as opposed to the one milking used in Single Gloucester. However, there are also those who say that it is so named because a traditional cheese was twice the size of a Single Gloucester. Originally, both cheeses were made from the milk of Gloucestershire cattle.

Double Gloucester has been creamery-made on a wide scale since World War 2, but farm-made cheeses are still available and are well worth seeking out. These have a thick, dry rind and are brined and dipped in lard, then bandaged or waxed.

Since the 18th century Double Gloucester has been coloured — first with beetroot or carrot juice, later with annatto — and in days gone by the rinds were painted with red dye to indicate that the cheese was richer and creamier than Single Gloucester. It was traditional to garland the cheeses with flowers and carry them through towns and villages at spring festivals.

Although this custom has long since died out, the ceremony of rolling a cheese down Cooper's Hill near Chipping Campden, in Gloucestershire, every Whit weekend still takes place.

Characteristics of the cheese are a close texture with a rounded, mellow flavour.

Pasteurised cows' milk. Creamery-made cheese widely available.

Appleby's Double Gloucester cheese.
Supplied by Neal's Yard Dairy;
Food Features

Flavoured versions include:

Abbeydale — onions and chives

Cotswold — onions and chives

County — layered with Stilton

Five Counties — Cheddar, Double Gloucester, Cheshire, Derby and Red Leicester in layers

Peppervale — finely chopped red and green peppers

Romany — Caerphilly and onions

Sherwood — sweet pickles

Farmhouse Double Gloucester
see Farmhouse Cheeses

Appleby's Double Gloucester
A pale-orange cheese with a light tangy flavour. Cloth-bound.
Appleby's of Hawkstone, near Whitchurch, Shropshire. Unpasteurised cows' milk. 4lb, 15lb and 30lb cylindricals.

Quicke's Double Gloucester
Firm-textured and moist with a deep-orange colour.
J. G. Quicke and Partners, Woodley, Devon. Pasteurised cows' milk. Vegetarian rennet.

Smart's Double Gloucester
Made from the farm's own herd of cows and ripened for seven months. Creamy and tangy.

Double Gloucester. *National Dairy Council*

D. H. & D. R. Smart, Old Ley Court, Birdwood, Gloucestershire. Unpasteurised cows' milk. Vegetarian rennet. 7–8lb.

Double Worcester

A smooth, slightly elastic full-fat cheese coloured orange with annatto. Hand-made to an original recipe (like all Ansteys cheeses), this smooth and tasty cheese is an interesting variation on Double Gloucester.

Ansteys of Worcester, Broomhall Farm, Worcester. Unpasteurised cows' milk. Vegetarian rennet. 6-8lb truckles and mini truckles.

Duddleswell

A full-fat hard cheese which is matured for a minimum of 12 weeks and has a natural rind. Smooth and creamy textured, it has a nice bite to it. Duddleswell is also available with

Duddleswell cheese. *Supplied by Jeroboam's; Food Features*

chives or with fresh peppercorns.

Sussex High Weald Dairy Sheep Products, Duddleswell, East Sussex. Unpasteurised sheep's milk. Vegetarian rennet. 1-2lb and 4-5lb traditional rounds.

Dunlop

A Scottish cheese similar to Cheddar and Double Gloucester, it was reputedly the first full-cream hard cheese to be made in Scotland. A woman from Ireland is thought to have developed the cheese in the late 17th century, and because it was so much nicer to eat than the hard cheeses hitherto made with skimmed milk, it soon began to be made on many other farms. However, by the 19th century factory production was introduced and the creamery-made cheese usually on offer today is a far cry from the traditional Dunlop, which is still available (see Dunloppe below). Pale in colour, it has a light, moist texture and a bland flavour.

Pasteurised cows' milk. Creamery-made cheese widely available.

Dunloppe

Traditionally made Dunlop.

Dunlop Dairy Products, Stewarton, Scotland. Pasteurised cows' milk.

Dunsyre Blue

This blue Scottish cheese comes from a farm in Lanarkshire and is made

Dunsyre Blue cheese. *Supplied by Paxton & Whitfield; Food Features*

from the milk of a single herd of Ayrshire cows grazed on rich pasture. Mould-ripened and semi-hard, it is a deliciously creamy cheese with a sharpish flavour.

H. J. Errington & Co, Ogscastle, Scotland. Unpasteurised cows' milk. Vegetarian rennet. 7lb wheels.

Dunwick

A soft, mild, unpressed cheese available with a number of flavourings which include black pepper, dill, herbs and garlic. Wrapped.

Seven Sisters Sheep Centre, East Dean, East Sussex. Pasteurised sheep's milk. Vegetarian rennet. 250gm.

Elgar

A hard traditional farmhouse cheese with a good flavour, having been matured for six months. Cloth-bound.

Richard Rogers, Malvern Cheesewrights, Lower Wick, Worcester. Unpasteurised cows' milk. Vegetarian rennet. 3-3.5lb wheels.

Elsdon

Smooth, slightly salty-flavoured hard cheese which softens with age.

Redesdale Dairy, Otterburn, Northumberland.

Pasteurised goats' milk. Vegetarian rennet. 2lb truckles, 6.5lb.

Emlett

A white, mould-ripened cheese with a strong, fruity taste. Creamy textured. Also sold fresh.

Sleight Farm, Timsbury, Avon. Unpasteurised sheep's milk. 5-6oz rounds.

Emlett cheese. *Supplied by Neal's Yard Dairy; Food Features*

Farmhouse Cheeses

Farmhouse Cheesemakers Ltd is a producers' co-operative. It was formed in 1988 from the membership of the Farmhouse Cheesemakers' Federations established in the late 1920s and early 1930s, and is committed to maintaining and perpetuating the craft of farmhouse cheesemaking through a strict approach to quality control and collective marketing through Mendip Foods Ltd.

Farmhouse Cheese is a generic name given to cheeses which are produced by members of the organisation. All the cheeses carry the Farmhouse logo, and must be produced by traditional methods on farms which use their own milk. The cheeses have to be assessed by an independent grader from the Milk Marketing Board Independent Farmhouse Cheese Grading Scheme at a given stage of production and only the top grades qualify. In this way the consumer can be assured that any cheese bearing the logo has been traditionally produced and is of the finest quality. This is not to say that the cheeses lose any of their individuality, as the same factors that cause variations in any farm-made cheese apply (see page 14).

Varieties of cheese carrying the Farmhouse logo include: Cheddar, Red and White Cheshire, Lancashire, Red Leicester, Double Gloucester, Caerphilly, Wensleydale and Derby.

Finn cheese. *Supplied by Neal's Yard Dairy; Food Features*

Finn

A new double-cream cheese from Neal's Yard.

Neal's Yard Creamery Ltd, Everlands Estate, Ide Hill, Kent. Unpasteurised cows' milk. Vegetarian rennet. 4oz rounds.

Flower Marie

A soft, creamy, mould-ripened cheese.

Greenacres Farm, near Lewes, East Sussex. Unpasteurised sheep's milk. Vegetarian rennet.

Fountains Gold

Made with milk taken from Jersey and Guernsey cows, this full-fat hard cheese is very rich and creamy.

Fountains Dairy Products, Kirkby Malzeard, North Yorkshire. Pasteurised cows' milk. Vegetarian rennet. 4.5lb half-wheel.

Fromage Frais

Literally meaning fresh cheese, this is a soft French cheese that is becoming increasingly popular in Britain.

Galic

A medium-fat, soft fresh cheese with fresh chopped garlic leaves and a coating of flaked hazelnuts.

Highland Fine Cheeses Ltd, Tain, Scotland. Pasteurised cows' milk. Unrenneted.

Flower Marie cheese. *Supplied by Neal's Yard Dairy; Food Features*

Galloway Goats

Hand-made from the milk of the farm's naturally fed and reared Saanen goats, this mild, creamy, moist and slightly crumbly cheese is waxed to retain its consistency and its flavour. As well as plain, an oak-smoked version is available.

California Farm, Newton Stewart, Wigtownshire, Scotland. Pasteurised goats' milk. Vegetarian rennet. 2.5lb.

Gedi

A range of small, individually wrapped soft cheeses.

Velde — a dumpy, truncated pyramid bloomy rind cheese coated with charcoal. Fresh and firm when young, it becomes stronger flavoured and almost runny with age.

Roubiulliac — fresh mild logs available plain, or with a coating of garlic, herbs or black pepper. St Gedi is a larger version, and is rolled in ash.

Chauvannes — resembles Camembert with its bloomy white crust and creamy inside.

Moillon — firm when young, it hardens with age. **Jouvenet** is the cylindrical-shaped version.

Crotton — small and cylindrical, this is made in the same style as the well-known French grilling cheese — Crottin.

Golden Cross cheese. *Supplied by Neal's Yard Dairy; Food Features*

Gedi Enterprises Ltd, Plumridge Farm, Barnet, Hertfordshire. Pasteurised goats' milk. Vegetarian rennet.

Gobhar

Gobhar is Gaelic for goat. This soft, mould-ripened cheese is mild but with a good flavour. Sold at two weeks old, it can be kept for up to four weeks. It is sold wrapped in waxed paper.

Highland Goat Products, Ballindalloch, Banffshire, Scotland. Unpasteurised goats' milk. Vegetarian rennet. 8oz rounds.

Golden Cross

A log-shaped mould-ripened soft cheese coated with ash. Made to a traditional St-Maure recipe, it is firm, creamy and fresh — slightly acidic-tasting.

Greenacres Farm, near Lewes, East Sussex. Unpasteurised goats' milk. Vegetarian rennet.

Gospel Green

Hand-made in the village of the same name, this fresh, tangy-tasting golden cheese has a natural grey rind and is cloth-bound. Spring and summer batches are softer and acquire a deeper colour.

Gospel Green Cottage, near Haslemere, Surrey. Unpasteurised cows' milk. Vegetarian rennet. 2lb, 4lb and 7lb truckles.

Gowrie

A hand-made, cloth-wrapped Cheddar.

Although firm-bodied, this is not a dense cheese. The flavour is smooth and lactic with a rich aftertaste. It is ripened on wooden slats.

Ingle Smokehouse, Perth, Scotland. Unpasteurised cows' milk. 60lb truckles.

Gruth Dhu

A blend of Crowdie and fresh double cream coated with peppercorns and oats. Dhu means black in Gaelic.

Highland Fine Cheeses Ltd, Tain, Scotland. Pasteurised cows' milk. Unrenneted.

Harbourne Blue

This is one of the few blue cheeses made from goats' milk; it comes from the same maker as Beenleigh Blue and is very similar. The name comes from the river near the valley in which it is matured. The goats are grazed on the

Harbourne Blue cheese. *Supplied by Neal's Yard Dairy; Food Features*

edge of Dartmoor and the cheese is available only seasonally.

Ticklemore Cheese, Totnes, Devon. Pasteurised goats' milk. 6lb wheels.

Gospel Green cheese. *Supplied by Neal's Yard Dairy; Food Features*

Hazlewood

A full-fat, semi-soft cheese from the Blackdown Goat Centre. Flavoured with garlic and parsley.

Blackdown Goat Centre, Devon. Goats' milk. Vegetarian rennet.

Hereford Hop

A hard cheese which has been matured in a coating of toasted hops. Mild and buttery in flavour, but the hops give a strong aroma.

Charles Martell & Son, Dymock, Gloucestershire. Pasteurised cows' milk. Vegetarian rennet. 4lb.

Hereford Hop

This semi-hard cheese of the same name as that made by Charles Martell is matured longer and is of a moister consistency. It is rich and creamy, with the hops giving it a distinctive appearance and delicate taste.
Malvern Cheesewrights, Lower Wick, Worcester. Unpasteurised cows' milk. Vegetarian rennet. 3-3.5lb wheel, 1.25lb truckle.

Herriot Farmhouse

A 19th-century recipe is used to make this unpressed, semi-hard cheese. Ripened in cloth for three months, it develops a nutty flavour and rough grey natural rind.
Shepherds Purse Cheeses, Thirsk, North Yorkshire. Pasteurised sheep's milk. Vegetarian rennet. 3lb and 7lb truckles.

Heydale

Heydale Mature is a washed-rind hard cheese with a strong tang.

Heydale Mellow is a firm, slightly elastic cheese with a slightly holey texture and a natural rind.
Heydale Cheeses, Chamberhouse Urbon Farm, East Heywood, Lancashire. Unpasteurised sheep's milk. Vegetarian rennet. 3-4lb.

Highland Crowdie

A long-established cheese unique to the Highlands and believed to pre-date the Vikings. For centuries it was widely made on Scottish farms and crofts and traditionally eaten for breakfast on oatcakes and topped with jam. It is a crumbly, low fat fresh cheese, simple and refreshing with a slightly acidic flavour. It should be eaten on the day of purchase.
Highland Fine Cheeses Ltd, Tain, Scotland. Pasteurised cows' milk. Rennet free.

Hramsa

A medium-fat spreading cheese mixed with chopped, fresh, locally picked wild garlic leaves and cream.
Highland Fine Cheeses Ltd, Tain, Scotland. Pasteurised cows' milk. Unrenneted.

Innes

A variety of soft cheeses marketed as Bosworth, Clifton and Button which are made from the milk of a herd of British Saanen goats. Sold fresh (three days), semi-matured (five days) or matured (14 days) either plain or coated with ash and dried herbs. Available singly or attractively packaged in small wooden boxes, they come in various sizes.
Highfields Dairy, Statfold, Staffordshire. Unpasteurised goats' milk. Vegetarian rennet.

Irthingspa

A semi-hard cheese with a fresh, tangy taste to it.
Irthingspa Dairy, Gilsland, Cumbria. Unpasteurised goats' milk. Vegetarian rennet. 1lb, 2lb and 5lb.

Isle of Mull

A very hard, dense cheese rather like Cheddar. It is hand-made in cloth-bound cylinders from the farm's herd of Ayrshire, Friesian and Jersey cows

Above: Gedi Cheeses.

Below: Innes Bosworth Leaf cheese.
Supplied by Paxton & Whitfield;
Food Features

and matured for at least eight months at the Tobermory Distillery.

Individually moulded 1lb cheeses, covered in dark green wax, are marketed as Tobermory Truckles.

Isle of Mull Flavells are mature Isle of Mull cheeses which have either been flavoured with mixed herbs, cracked black pepper, caraway seeds, Mull mustard, or smoked.
Jeff Reade, Isle of Mull, Scotland. Unpasteurised cows' milk. 55lb drums and 1lb truckles.

Jersey Blue
A full-fat, soft creamy blue cheese made from the milk of Jersey cows grazed on the Brendon Hills. Can be kept for up to six weeks.
Exmoor Blue Cheeses, Willett Farm Dairy, Lydeard St Lawrence, Somerset.

Unpasteurised cows' milk. Vegetarian rennet. 2-3.5lb.

Jervaulx
A plain soft cheese covered in clear wax.
Fortmayne Farm Dairy, Bedale, North Yorkshire. Pasteurised cows' milk. 1-1.25lb rounds.

Kelsae
A relatively new cheese made from the full cream milk of the farm's herd of Jersey cows to an old recipe. Yoghurt made on the farm is used as a starter. Matured for at least four months, Kelsae is similar to Wensleydale in texture, but creamier.
Stichill Jerseys, Kelso, Scotland. Unpasteurised cows' milk. 2.5-13lb drums.

Lanark Blue
A soft, strongly-flavoured creamy-textured blue-veined cheese from Lanark with a salty tang. *H. J. Errington & Co, Ogscastle, Scotland. Unpasteurised sheep's milk. Vegetarian rennet.*

Lanark Blue cheese. *Supplied by Jeroboam's; Food Features*

Lancashire

This was first made in the Fylde area of Lancashire and came about because the farmers did not have very much milk to spare each day so the curds from both morning and evening milkings were combined with curds from the previous day before being salted and milled and transferred to moulds to mature in the farmhouse kitchens.

Despite being very labour intensive, large quantities of Lancashire were traditionally made by farmers' wives, and it became a staple food for mill workers. In 1913 the first creamery began making Lancashire to meet the demand and since then factory-made cheese has flooded the market. Traditionally made, this is a moist, flaky cheese with an acidic, slightly salty flavour. It becomes smoother and more flavoursome with age and is an excellent cheese for melting and crumbling.

Pasteurised cows' milk. Creamery-made cheese widely available.

Farmhouse Lancashire see Farmhouse Cheeses

Kirkham's Lancashire

Curds are taken from three consecutive days' milkings to make this cheese and as a result it has a very distinctive, complex flavour. Firm, crumbly and moist with a real bite.

Beesley Farm, Goosnargh, Lancashire. Unpasteurised milk. 4lb, 20lb and 45lb.

Sandham's Lancashire

Traditionally made Lancashire cheese.

Soft, sweet and buttery. Also available with garlic or sage.

J. J. Sandham Ltd, Barton, Lancashire. Pasteurised cows' milk. Vegetarian rennet.

Leafield

A hard cheese with the smooth consistency of Cheddar and a good tang to it.

Rodney Whitworth, West Hanney, Oxfordshire. Pasteurised sheep's milk. Vegetarian rennet. 4lb truckles.

Leicester see Red Leicester

Little Derby

This hard cheese is made to a traditional recipe that had not been used for over 50 years. After maturing for seven months, during which time the cheese acquires a tasty flavour, it is washed in red wine.

Fowlers of Earlswood, Earlswood, West Midlands. Pasteurised cows' milk. Vegetarian and non vegetarian rennet. 28lb whole cheeses and 7lb quarters.

Little Rydings

Wrapped Camembert-like cheese with a bloomy rind that tends to speckle.

Sleight Farm, Timsbury, Avon. Unpasteurised sheep's milk. 5oz and 7oz rounds.

Llanboidy

This full-fat, hard pressed cheese is made with the milk of the rare Red Poll cow and as such is unique not only in Britain but in the world. Creamy textured with a natural rind,

t can be eaten from two to ten
months of age.

A version with added laverbread is
also made.

*Llanboidy Cheesemakers, Whitland,
Dyfed, Wales. Unpasteurised cows'
milk. 10lb rounds.*

Llangloffan

Semi-hard full-fat cheese organically
made from grass-fed Jersey cows'
milk in Pembrokeshire. Rather like a
creamy Cheshire with a crumbly
texture and a natural rind,
Llangloffan comes plain, or red with
chives and garlic. The cheese tends to
be made while the cows are grazing,
so it is not widely available between
February and May. It is sold at two
months old and at five to six months
when it has developed a stronger
flavour.

Visitors are welcome at the farm.
*Llangloffan Farmhouse Cheese,
Castle Morris, Dyfed, Wales.
Unpasteurised cows' milk Vegetarian
rennet. 4lb, 9lb and 25lb drums.*

Loddiswell Banon

Unpressed medium-fat soft fresh
cheese available plain or with garlic
and covered with parsley. Made at
the Blackdown Goat Centre.
*Blackdown Farm, Loddiswell,
Devon. Unpasteurised goats' milk.
Vegetarian rennet. 2oz rounds.*

Opposite: Lancashire.
National Dairy Council

Above: Little Rydings cheese.
*Supplied by Neal's Yard Dairy; Food
Features*

Malvern

Based on the original recipe for Wensleydale cheese, which was traditionally made from sheep's milk in the 17th century, this semi-hard cheese has a smooth texture and subtle flavour with a hint of nuttiness.

Malvern Cheesewrights, Lower Wick, Worcester. Unpasteurised sheep's milk. Vegetarian rennet. 3.5lb and 5.5lb wheels, 1lb truckles.

Meldon see Curworthy

Mendip

This firm cheese is made in a round basket mould and matured for two to eight months. Slightly acidic with a fruity tang, it becomes stronger and harder with age. Ivory in colour, it is characterised by small holes (eyes) and an almost spongy texture. The natural, brownish-yellow oiled rind should not be cracked or wrinkled. Summer cheeses are drier, but excellent for cooking.

Sleight Farm, Timsbury, Avon. Unpasteurised goats' milk. 4-6lb.

Merlin cheeses

A range of hard, Cheddar-type cheeses made organically from the farm's own herd of goats. The varieties, each waxed in a different colour, include walnut, olive, pineapple, apricot, ginger, celery, apple and smoked. Mature and mild versions of most varieties available. The cheeses are vacuum packed so will keep indefinitely.

Merlin Cheeses, Pontrhydygroes, Dyfed, Wales. Unpasteurised goats' milk. Vegetarian rennet. 2lb and 0.5lb minis.

Nanny's Cheddar

A pleasantly flavoured Cheddar cheese. Widely available and useful for those allergic to cows' milk.

Cricket Malherbie Farms Ltd, Nether Stowey, Somerset. Pasteurised goats' milk. Vegetarian rennet.

Nepicar

The makers of Nepicar claim that this was the first cheese to be made from pasteurised sheep's milk in the United Kingdom. It is a hard, pale yellow cheese which improves as it matures and becomes creamier. It has a natural rind.

British Sheep Dairy Products, Wrotham Heath, Kent. Pasteurised sheep's milk. Vegetarian rennet. 16 24oz rounds, 4.5-6lb.

Newbury

Full-fat, semi-hard rindless cheese. Mild and creamy, it is available plain or with fresh garlic and rolled in mixed herbs.

Hollam Hill Farm Products, Titchfield, Hampshire. Unpasteurised cows' milk. Vegetarian rennet. 8in wheel (3lb).

Northumberland

A smooth-textured hard cheese matured for at least ten weeks.

Redesdale Dairy, Otterburn, Northumberland. Pasteurised cows' milk. Vegetarian rennet.

Nuns of Caen

A washed rind, soft cheese with a fruity flavour. Produced in the manner originated by nuns from Caen in Normandy who founded the village of Minchinhampton.

Charles Martell & Son, Dymock, Gloucestershire. Unpasteurised sheep's milk. Vegetarian rennet. 4lb rounds.

Olde York

This cheese is made to an original York recipe, using the Coulommiers method of manufacture. Creamy and soft with a subtle flavour, it comes plain or with either chives, green peppercorns, garlic and parsley, or mint. Each is covered in a different coloured wax coating.
Shepherds Purse Cheeses, Thirsk, North Yorkshire. Pasteurised sheep's milk. Vegetarian rennet. 1lb truckles, halves and quarters.

Old Sussex

This is a hard-pressed cheese that has been described as a cross between Cheddar and Cheshire in texture. Matured for six to eight months with a natural rind, it has a good, strong, distinctive flavour of its own.

A smoked version — Sussex Smokey — is slightly younger, allowing the smoked flavour to be enjoyed without competition. It is rindless, vacuum packed and a lovely golden brown colour.

Scrumpy Sussex , again rindless and vacuum packed, has cider, garlic and mixed herbs added to it.
Turners Dairies, Patching, West Sussex. Unpasteurised cows' milk. Vegetarian rennet. Old Sussex 8-9lb wheel; Sussex Smokey and Scrumpy Sussex 3-4lb half-moons.

Old Worcester White

This pale yellow, creamy cheese with the texture of Cheddar — although rather softer — has a really good bite to it which lingers. The rind is a thin natural one, the cheese having been matured in calico bandages.
Ansteys of Worcester, Broomhall Farm, Worcester. Unpasteurised cows' milk. Vegetarian rennet. 6-8lb truckles and mini truckles.

Orkney

A hard, close-textured cheese now largely factory-made at Kirkwall, although some is made traditionally on farms in the Orkneys. The creamery variety is widely available. It comes plain, coloured with annatto or smoked, and keeps well.
Pasteurised cows' milk.

Orkney cheese.
Supplied by Neal's Yard Dairy; Food Features

Pant-ysgawn Farm

A soft cheese originally made on a farm in the Brecon Beacons National Park, now made to the same recipe on a dairy near Abergavenny. Produced in small rounds and sold whole or sliced, it is mild, not at all 'goaty', clean-tasting and easy to spread. Comes coated with peppercorns, herbs or peppers.
Abergavenny Fine Foods, Abergavenny, Gwent, Wales. Pasteurised goats' milk. Vegetarian rennet.

Pencarreg

An organically produced, full-fat soft cheese with a bloomy rind. Moist and chalky at first, it becomes softer and runnier with age and develops a very distinctive flavour. Best in summer, when it is a deep gold colour.

Pencarreg Blue

is a new soft blue cheese.
Welsh Organic Foods Ltd, Lampeter, Dyfed, Wales. Pasteurised cows' milk. Vegetarian rennet. 10oz boxed rounds, 3lb oval.

Perroche

Medium-fat soft cheese that must be eaten immediately. It is sold within three days of being made. Clean, goaty taste with a hint of almonds. Comes plain or rolled in fresh herbs.
Neal's Yard Creamery Ltd, Everlands Estate, Ide Hill, Kent.

Unpasteurised goats' milk. Vegetarian rennet. 4oz rounds, 1lb logs.

Pyramid

A strong flavoured, full-fat soft cheese coated with ash.
Nut Knowle Farm, Woodmancote, West Sussex. Pasteurised goats' milk. Vegetarian rennet.

Quantock Blue

A full-fat, soft blue cheese hand-made chiefly from milk from the Quantock Sheep Milking centre at Nether Stowey at the foot of the Quantock Hills. Keeps for up to six weeks if refrigerated.
Exmoor Blue Cheeses, Willett Farm Dairy, Lydeard St Lawrence,

Perroche cheese, rosemary, dill and tarragon. *Supplied by Neal's Yard Dairy; Food Features*

Pyramid cheese. *Supplied by
Paxton & Whitfield; Food Features*

*Somerset. Unpasteurised sheep's
milk. Vegetarian rennet. 3.5-4.5lb.*

Quark
The name means curds in German. It
is a low-fat soft cheese, smooth
textured and slightly acidic.

Ragstone
A creamy log of soft cheese.
*Neal's Yard Creamery Ltd, Everlands
Estate, Ide Hill, Kent. Unpasteurised
goats' milk. Vegetarian rennet.*

Redesdale
A full-fat hard cheese. Smooth and
sweetish tasting.
*Redesdale Dairy, Otterburn,
Northumberland. Pasteurised
sheep's milk. Vegetarian rennet.*

Red Cheshire see Cheshire

Red Leicester
A cheese widely known by its deep
reddish colour obtained from annatto
(formerly from carrot and beetroot
juice). Annatto was banned for a time
and when reintroduced the cheese

Ragstone cheese. *Supplied by Neal's Yard Dairy; Food Features*

became known as Red Leicester to differentiate it from the former paler version, which now no longer exists.

This is the only cheese still made from a range of local cheeses produced in the Shires, Kington cheese from Nottingham and the cheeses from Lincolnshire and Suffolk having disappeared. Blue Leicester, too, is no longer made; this was often made on the creameries that produced Stilton.

Farm-made Red Leicester is produced in large, flat, round shapes and has a thin, dry rind. It has a close, flaky texture and a delicate, sweet flavour which strengthens with ageing.

It is a good melting cheese and is traditionally served with watercress. Flavoured variations include:

Beauchamp — herbs and garlic

Cromwell — layered with Derby

Walgrove — walnuts
Pasteurised cows' milk. Creamery-made cheese widely available.

Farmhouse Red Leicester see Farmhouse Cheeses

Ribblesdale cheeses
Lightly pressed and wax-finished in different colours, these creamy, mild cheeses are hand-made in the old Dales style to a traditional recipe

with either cows', ewes' or goats' milk. All are also available with garlic, or oak-smoked. They can be kept for up to two years.

Ribblesdale Cheesemakers, Ashes Farm, Horton-in-Ribblesdale, North Yorkshire. Pasteurised cows' milk, sheep's and goats' milk. Vegetarian rennet. 4lb wheels.

Rosary Plain

A soft and creamy cheese with a mild flavour. It is also available with garlic and herbs.

Rosary Goats Cheese, Landford, Wiltshire. Unpasteurised goats' milk. Vegetarian rennet.

Sage Derby see Derby

St George

A full-fat, Camembert-type cheese made from the milk of the farm's own flock of Toggenberg goats.

Nut Knowle Farm, Woodmancote, West Sussex. Pasteurised goats' milk. Vegetarian rennet.

St Illtyd

This strong, very distinctive-tasting Cheddar-type cheese is blended with white wine, garlic and herbs, which

Rosary cheese. *Supplied by Neal's Yard Dairy; Food Features*

give it a speckled appearance. The larger cheeses come black-waxed, and the smaller ones are wrapped in muslin. Excellent for grilling or melting.

Abergavenny Fine Foods, Abergavenny, Gwent, Wales. Pasteurised cows' milk. Vegetarian rennet.

Scottish Cheddar see Cheddar

Scrumpy Sussex see Old Sussex

Severn Sisters

A reduced fat, softish cheese with a sharp, tangy flavour. Matured vacuum packed, it is sold green-waxed.

Richard Rogers, Malvern Cheesewrights, Lower Wick, Worcester. Unpasteurised cows' milk. Vegetarian rennet. 2lb.

Sharpham

An excellent, Brie-type creamy cheese made from Jersey cows' milk. Matured for three weeks, it has a white surface mould and a full, distinctive flavour. Available seasonally.

Sharpham Creamery, Totnes, Devon. Unpasteurised cows' milk. Vegetarian rennet. 1lb and 2lb cylinders.

Shropshire Blue

The origin of this cheese's name is a bit of a mystery, as it has never had anything to do with Shropshire. It

Sharpham cheese. *Supplied by Neal's Yard Dairy; Food Features*

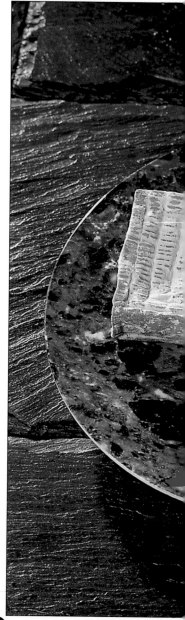

Shropshire Blue. *Supplied by Neal's Yard Dairy; Food Features*

was first produced in Scotland but the dairy there closed and now it is made at dairies in Nottinghamshire and Leicestershire. Easily recognised by its bright orange colouring with blue veining, this is a creamy unpressed cheese not unlike Blue Cheshire, but somewhat richer. It keeps well.

Pasteurised cows' milk. Colston Bassett Dairy, Colston Bassett, Nottingham.

Single Gloucester

This dates back to the 8th century and was originally made from the milk of Old Gloucester cows; having almost completely died out, it is now enjoying something of a revival. It has a lower fat content than Double Gloucester as some of the cream is skimmed off to give a lighter, more crumbly texture and although of a milder flavour, Single Gloucester still has an edge to it. Unlike Double Gloucester, it is not coloured.

J. G. Quicke and Partners, Woodley, Devon. Pasteurised cows' milk. Vegetarian rennet.

D. H. & D. R. Smart, Old Ley Court, Birdwood, Gloucestershire. Unpasteurised cows' milk. Vegetarian rennet.

Charles Martell & Son, Dymock, Gloucestershire. Pasteurised cows' milk. Vegetarian rennet.

Spenwood cheese. *Supplied by Neal's Yard Dairy; Food Features*

Skirrid

Full-fat, hard Caerphilly-type pressed cheese which is marinated in mead for 24hr before being matured.
Little Acorn Products, Bethania, Dyfed, Wales. Unpasteurised sheep's milk. Vegetarian rennet. 5-5.5lb.

Sleight

Full-fat, moist, fresh cheese available plain or coated with rosemary, pepper, or herbs and garlic.

Sleight Farm, Timsbury, Avon. Unpasteurised goats' milk. Vegetarian rennet. 4oz rounds.

Somerset Blue

Hand-made from the milk of two Jersey herds grazed on the lower slopes of the Brendon Hills, this full-fat, hard unpressed blue cheese is firm and rich-textured. It can be kept for up to two months.
Exmoor Blue Cheeses, Willett Farm Dairy, Lydeard St Lawrence, Somerset. Unpasteurised cows' milk. Vegetarian rennet. 4.5-5.5lb and vacuum packed in smaller quantities.

Somerset Brie

Made to a traditional French recipe, this cheese develops a full flavour with age.

Somerset Camembert is made by the same company.
Lubborn Cheese Ltd, Crewkerne, Somerset. Pasteurised cows' milk. 5lb wheels.

Spenwood

This is made at Spencer's Wood in Berkshire — hence the name — and comes with a greyish-brown natural rind or a waxed finish. Smooth and firm textured, Spenwood is matured for three months and has a deep, rounded flavour — although it is not overly strong.
Village Maid Cheese, Spencer's Wood, Berkshire. Unpasteurised sheep's milk. Vegetarian rennet. 5lb traditionals.

Staffordshire Organic

As its name suggests, this is an organically-made cheese, and it is similar to Cheddar. Traditionally bound and matured in cylinders for three months, it comes plain, with chives or with mixed herbs and wild garlic. It can also be made without salt on request.
M. & B. Deaville, Acton, Staffordshire. Unpasteurised cows' milk. Vegetarian rennet.

Stichill

Made from the rich milk of Jersey cows, this is a mild crumbly cheese after the style of Cheshire.
Stichill Jerseys, Kelso, Scotland. Unpasteurised cows' milk.

Stilton

The true origins of Stilton are unclear, but it has more or less been established that in the early 18th century a housekeeper at Quenby Hall, near Leicester, taught herself to make the cheese we now know as Stilton from a recipe entitled Lady Beaumont's Cheese. Where Lady Beaumont obtained this recipe is less certain, however. What is known is that Elizabeth Scarbrow (the housekeeper) began to sell her cheeses to a relative who owned the Bell Inn at Stilton, in Huntingdonshire — now Cambridgeshire — and thus the cheese acquired its name, and its fame began.

In time the cheese began to be made by other farmers in the region, but it was an extremely lengthy and troublesome business and by 1910 those producing Stilton collaborated with a view to improving and defining the process. Nearly 60 years later these definitions were given legal backing and inferior cheeses hitherto masquerading under the name of Stilton were ousted. Now, the King of English Cheese must be made from full-cream milk produced by herds grazed in the counties of Leicestershire, Nottinghamshire and Derbyshire only. It must be made in cylindrical form with no applied

Stilton. *National Dairy Council*

pressure and allowed to form its own crust. Both the name STILTON and the method of manufacture are registered certification trade marks.

Good Stilton is characterised by a creamy yellow colour with greeny-blue veins spreading evenly out to the crust from the centre. The crust should be dry, firm and without any cracks, although the colour and texture can vary. Light veining indicates the cheese is young and therefore milder than a cheese with strong veining.

White Stilton is young Stilton that has not yet formed any blue veining. It has a less tangy flavour and is generally of a crumblier consistency with scarcely any crust.

When buying a whole Stilton, do so from a reputable seller who keeps his cheeses well and will allow you to taste a sample from the cheese you are buying. If the cheese is not going to be used all at once, cut off the top crust and retain. Then cut off a circle about 3in thick and cut it into wedges. Replace the crust on the whole Stilton.

When buying pre-packed portions make sure that there is no browning or wrinkling. Stilton keeps fairly well in the fridge, and can be frozen for up to three months; White Stilton should be eaten as soon as possible after purchase and should not be kept for more than a couple of days in the fridge.

The practice of scooping or soaking Stilton in port is now frowned upon as being wasteful of both the cheese and the port.

A traditional whole cheese weighs 15lb and sizes down to 5oz wedges are available. Pottery jars are also available, particularly at Christmas. Along with other blue cheeses, Stilton is a very versatile cooking cheese.

Flavoured versions include:

Admiral — Cheddar cheese and port

County — layered with Double Gloucester

Walton — Cheddar and chopped walnuts

White Stilton with apricot— White Stilton blended with chives and onions
Leicestershire, Derbyshire and Nottinghamshire. Pasteurised cows' milk.

Stinking Bishop

The name should give some clue to the latest addition to Charles Martell's stable of good cheeses. Not for those who dislike pungent smells, this full-fat rind-washed soft cheese is steeped in perry and has a strong taste to match its aroma.
Charles Martell & Son, D y m o c k , Gloucestershire. Pasteurised cows' milk. Vegetarian rennet. 4-5lb.

Sussex Slipcote

The recipe for this full-fat, soft cheese dates back to Shakespeare's day. Moist and rindless, with a light, creamy flavour, it is packed in small wooden boxes. Also available with herbs and garlic or cracked peppercorns.
Sussex High Weald Dairy Sheep Products, Duddleswell, East Sussex. Unpasteurised sheep's milk. Vegetarian rennet. 4oz rounds and 2lb roll.

Sussex Slipcote cheese.
Supplied by Jeroboam's; Food Features

Sussex Smokey see Old Sussex

Swaledale Cheese

A soft, close-textured white cheese — not unlike a moister version of Wensleydale — that came over with the Norman monks. Up until the 17th century, when cows were introduced to the Dales, it was made with sheep's milk. Jersey cows reared in the dale now provide the milk. Creamy and mild but with a distinctive flavour, the cheese is matured for three to four weeks and is either left to develop a natural rind, or it is waxed.

Varieties available are:

Chives and garlic

Applemint Swaledale

Old Peculier — the curds are soaked in Theakston's Old Peculier ale (4fl oz to every lb of curd) giving the cheese a marbled appearance. Lightly pressed and black-waxed, it has a soft texture and a unique flavour.

Richmond Smoked — oak and applewood chippings are used to smoke the cheese, before maturing for three weeks. Comes red-waxed.

The Swaledale Cheese Co, Richmond, North Yorkshire. Unpasteurised cows' milk 1lb and 6lb discs.

Swaledale Ewes

This is a revival of the original Swaledale recipe, using sheep's milk. Light, creamy and moist, it has more body than the cows' milk cheese.

The Swaledale Cheese Co, Richmond, North Yorkshire. Unpasteurised sheep's milk.

Swaledale cheese. *Supplied by Paxton & Whitfield; Food Features*

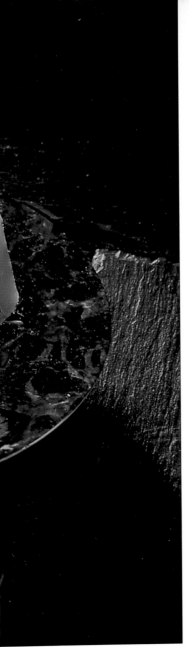

Tala cheese. *Supplied by Jeroboam's; Food Features*

Swinzie

A hard-pressed pale yellow cheese with a good flavour.

Dunlop Dairy Products, Stewarton, Scotland. Pasteurised sheep's milk. Vegetarian rennet. 4lb rounds and vacuum packed.

Tala

A dense cheese with a mild, creamy taste to it and some veining. A certain amount of the smaller cheeses are now available smoked.

North Beer Farm, Boyton, Cornwall. Unpasteurised sheep's milk. Vegetarian rennet. 1lb and 5lb.

Teifi

Made organically in Wales, using low sodium salt, this Gouda-style cheese is rich and creamy with a strong flavour. The smaller sizes are produced with a yellow wax coating.

Flavourings include chives, garlic, garlic and onion, celery garlic, sweet pepper, cumin seeds, mustard seed, nettles and seaweed. Good for fondues and melting. A maturer version, plain only, is also available.

Glynhynod Organic Farmers, Llandysul, Dyfed, Wales. Unpasteurised cows' milk. Vegetarian rennet. All varieties: 1lb minis, 2lb and 10lb. Plain only, 20lb.

Teviotdale

Made from the milk of the farm's pedigree Jersey cows, this full-fat hard cheese has a distinct, slightly salty taste. It ripens slightly with age, and may develop brown patches as it does so.

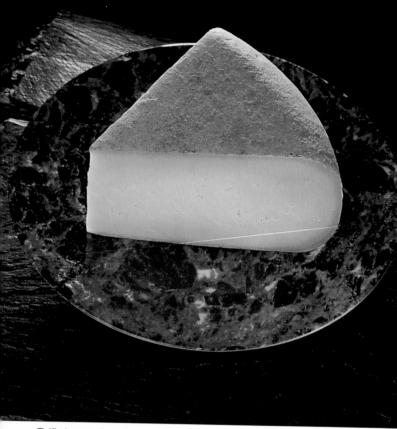

Teifi cheese. *Supplied by Jeroboam's; Food Features*
Easter Weens, Bonchester, Scotland. Unpasteurised cows' milk. 2.5lb truckles.

Thistledown

A soft, creamy — almost spreadable — cheese. Mild tasting and not goaty, the cheeses are coated in yellow wax.
Town Head Farm, Askwith, near Otley, North Yorkshire. Unpasteurised goats' milk. Vegetarian rennet. 3-4lb and 10oz individuals.

Ticklemore Goat

Semi-hard cheese hand pressed into flat round basket moulds and matured for at least 10 weeks. Rich and strongly flavoured. The natural rind shows moulding.
Ticklemore Cheese, Totnes, Devon. Pasteurised goats' milk.

Opposite: Ticklemore cheese.
Supplied by Neal's Yard Dairy; Food Features

Tobermory see Isle of Mull

Tornegus

This Caerphilly-type cheese is made by R. A. Duckett in Somerset then, when just two days old, it is transferred to Surrey where it is washed in a concoction of wine from the Penshurst Vineyard in Kent, brine and herbs and matured. The result is a very distinctive, sharply flavoured, creamy cheese with an orange rind.

James Aldridge, Rooks Farm, near Godstone, Surrey. Unpasteurised cows' milk cheese. Vegetarian rennet.

Torville

Young Duckett's Caerphilly rind-washed in local cider which imparts a strong flavour to the cheese.

R. A. Duckett & Co Ltd, Wedmore, Somerset. Unpasteurised cows' milk. Vegetarian rennet.

Tymsboro' soft cheese. *Supplied by Neal's Yard Dairy; Food Features*

Tymsboro'

Produced as a squat pyramid, this medium-fat cheese has a thin bloomy rind. Sometimes ash-coated. Very creamy near the rind; chalky and dense in the middle. Strong and slightly sweet tasting.
Sleight Farm, Timsbury, Avon. Unpasteurised goats' milk. Vegetarian rennet. 9-10oz pyramids.

Tyn Grug

Full-fat, hard pressed Cheddar-like cheese. Rich and creamy with a peppery tang. Seasonally available.
Tyn Grug, Lampeter, Dyfed, Wales. Unpasteurised cows' milk. Microbial rennet. 6lb, 18lb and 36lb cylindricals.

Tynedale Spa

A semi-hard cheese made to a traditional Dales recipe. Creamy, mild and crumbly.

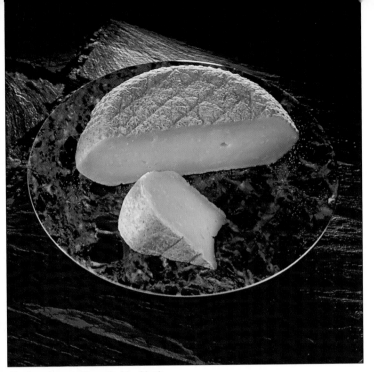

Tyning cheese. *Supplied by Neals Yard Dairy; Food Features*

Irthingspa Dairy, Gilsland, Cumbria. Unpasteurised cows' milk. Vegetarian rennet. 1lb, 2lb and 5lb.

Tyning
Made on the same farm as Mendip and with the same basket-moulded rind. Very close-textured, hard and flavoursome.
Sleight Farm, Timsbury, Avon. Unpasteurised sheep's milk. 6-8lb.

Vulscombe
This full-fat unrenneted cheese is hand-made in small rounds. Fresh and creamy, the lightly pressed curd also comes with fresh herbs and garlic or garlic and peppercorns.
Vulscombe Cheese, Higher Vulscombe, near Tiverton, Devon. Unpasteurised goats' milk. Unrenneted. 6oz cylindricals.

Walda
Made to a traditional Gouda recipe, this cheese has an elastic but firm texture with a fruity tang.
Wield Wood Sheep Dairy, near Alresford, Hampshire. Unpasteurised sheep's milk. 2lb, 4.5lb and 6.5lb. Gouda shape.

Waterloo

This golden-coloured cheese has a soft orange natural rind. It is tangy and peppery in flavour.
Village Maid Cheese, Spencer's Wood, Berkshire. Unpasteurised cows' milk. Vegetarian rennet.

Wealden Round

Medium fat, soft, moist fresh cheese from the Weald of Kent. Available with a variety of fresh herbs and spices — tarragon, parsley, garlic, black pepper, chives, spring onions. It is sold within three days of making and should be eaten immediately.
Neal's Yard Creamery, Everlands Estate, Ide Hill, Kent. Unpasteurised cows' milk. Vegetarian rennet. 9oz rounds.

Waterloo cheese. *Supplied by Neal's Yard Dairy; Food Features*

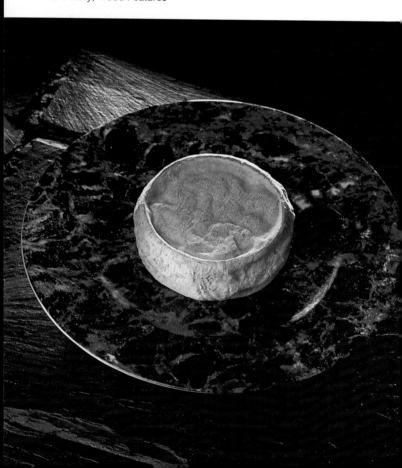

Wealden cheese. *Supplied by Neal's Yard Dairy; Food Features*

Wedmore

A Caerphilly-type cheese with a band of fresh chopped chives running though the centre. The mild, lactic flavour strengthens with age. A smoked version is also available.
R. A. Duckett & Co Ltd, Wedmore, Somerset. Unpasteurised cows' milk. Vegetarian rennet. 4.5lb discs.

Wellington

Made from the milk of the Duke of Wellington's pedigree Guernsey herd, this deep-yellow full-fat cheese has a natural grey rind. Rich and creamy, with a sweet, almost fruity flavour. Made by Village Maid of Spencer's Wood, the cheeses are matured at Stratfield Saye, the Duke of Wellington's home, for six months.

Wellington cheese. *Supplied by Neal's Yard Dairy; Food Features*

Stratfield Saye, Hampshire. Unpasteurised cows' milk. Vegetarian rennet. 2lb, 5lb and 10lb.

Wensleydale

Wensleydale was first made as a blue-veined cheese in the Yorkshire Dales from a recipe originating from the French monks who settled in the area at the time of the Norman Conquest. Sheep's milk was used up until the mid-17th century, when Shorthorn cows took over as the main source of milk. Traditionally soft, creamy, moist and open-textured with a delicate piquancy, Blue Wensleydale is now made in limited quantities and the white variety, crumbly and creamy white in appearance with a clean, sharp, slightly salty flavour, is now far more widely available, most of it being creamery-made.

The creamery at Hawes was the first factory to be established in the

Dales and it is still making a number of cheeses, including cloth-bound Wensleydale.

Traditionally, Wensleydale is eaten in the Dales with apple pie, fruit cake or gingerbread. Usually sold at about a month old, it does not improve with age and should be eaten within a few days of purchase. *Pasteurised cows' milk. Creamery-made cheese widely available.*

Farmhouse Wensleydale see
Farmhouse Cheeses

King Richard III Wensleydale
Hand-made cheeses made from the milk of cows reared in Wensleydale itself and wrapped in muslin. *Fortmayne Farm Dairy, Bedale, North Yorkshire. Pasteurised cows' milk.*

Real Wensleydale
Based on an old Wensleydale recipe, this unusual full-fat cheese is made from a mixture of cows' and sheep's milk. *Cloth-bound.*

Wensleydale.*National Dairy Council*

Redesdale Dairy, Otterburn, Northumberland. Pasteurised/unpasteurised cows' and sheep's milk. 2lb and 8lb truckles.

Wensleydale
Made from ewes' milk in the traditional way, this semi-hard, rather flaky cheese has a clean, sharp flavour.
Shepherds Purse Cheeses, Thirsk, North Yorkshire. Pasteurised sheep's milk. Vegetarian rennet. 10-13oz baby cheeses and 3-4lb cutting cheeses.

White Stilton see Stilton

Wigmore
Named after the cheesemakers, this is a white, soft, slightly oily natural-rind cheese with the same sort of texture as Brie. Mildly flavoured with a sweetish taste and a typical 'wet-wool' aroma.
Village Maid Cheese, Spencer's Wood, Berkshire. Unpasteurised sheep's milk. Vegetarian rennet. 1lb and 3-4lb.

Worcestershire Gold
Made from the milk of Jersey cows which graze on the pastures of Sandwell Priory, where cheese was formerly made by Cistercian monks, this semi-hard, bright-golden coloured cheese is rich and creamy with a clean aftertaste. Slightly sweet and full of flavour.
Malvern Cheesewrights, Lower Wick, Worcester. Unpasteurised cows' milk.

Vegetarian rennet. 3.5lb and 5.5lb wheels, 1lb truckles.

Worcestershire Sauce Cheese
As might be expected, the overriding flavour of this cheese is that of the Worcestershire Sauce and Lea & Perrins Original which is added to the milled curds. The pale yellow cheese is marbled with light brown and it has a very thin natural rind.
Ansteys of Worcester, Broomhall Farm, Worcester. Unpasteurised cows' milk. Vegetarian rennet. 6-8lb truckles and mini truckles.

Yorkshire Blue
Similar to a young Wensleydale when young. Crumbly and flaky with a mild taste, this blue cheese acquires a softness and creaminess with age and a strong, though not sharp, flavour.
Shepherds Purse Cheeses, Thirsk, North Yorkshire. Pasteurised sheep's milk. Vegetarian rennet. 8lb.

Yorkshire Lowlands Farmhouse Cheese
A bright-red wax coating covers this hard-pressed white cheese which is matured from three to six months. Rich and full-bodied, it has a nutty, woody taste to it.
Shepherds Purse Cheeses, Thirsk, North Yorkshire. Pasteurised sheep's milk. Vegetarian rennet. 10-12oz and 3-4lb.

Yorvik

A soft cheese with an orange stripe
and chives running through it.
*Fortmayne Farm Dairy, Bedale,
North Yorkshire.*
Pasteurised cows' milk.
1-1.25lb rounds.

Wigmore cheese. *Supplied by Neal's
Yard Dairy; Food Features*

Cheese Shops

Most of the following retailers are members of the Specialist Cheesemakers' Association (see page 96).

ENGLAND

Avon
Paxton & Whitfield,
1 John Street, Bath, Avon BA1 2JL.
Tel: 0225 46640

The Fine Cheese Co,
29 Walcot Street, Bath, Avon BA1 5BN.

Buckinghamshire
The Cheeseman,
Chenies, Nags Head Lane, Great Missenden, Bucks HP16 0HG.

Cheshire
Godfrey Williams and Son,
Corner House, 9/11 The Square, Sandbach, Cheshire CW11 0AP.

The Cheese Shop,
116 Northgate Street, Chester CH1 2HT.

The Good Food Shop,
68 Chestergate, Macclesfield, Cheshire SK11 6DY.

Cumbria
Butterworth's Fine Foods,
50 Quarry Rigg, Bowness-on-Windermere, Cumbria LA23 3DT.

J. J. Graham,
Fisher Street, Carlisle, Cumbria.

J. J. Graham,
Finkle Street, Kendal, Cumbria LA9 4AB.

J. J. Graham,
Market Place, Penrith, Cumbria.

The Barn Shop and Tea Room,
Low Sizergh Farm, Kendal, Cumbria LA8 8AE.

The Cheese Larder,
Market Hall, Kendal, Cumbria.

Derbyshire
Chatsworth Farm Shop,
Stud Farm, Pilsley, Derbys DE45 1UH.

Pugsons,
Cliff House, Terrace Road, Buxton, Derbys SK17 6DR.

St James Delicatessen,
9/11 St James Street, Derby DE1 1QT.

Devon
Ticklemore Cheese
1 Ticklemore Street, Totnes, Devon

Watty's Delicatessen,
16 Catherine Street, Exeter, Devon EX1 1EU.

Dorset
Sabins Fine Foods,
5 Hound Street, Sherborne, Dorset DT9 3AB.

Gloucestershire
Birdwood House Farm,
Birdwood, Huntley, Glos GL19 3EJ.

Number One Foodhalls,
The Market Place, Cirencester, Glos GL7 2PE.

Greater Manchester
The Cheese Hamlet,
706 Wilmslow Road, Didsbury, Manchester M20 0DW.

Hampshire
Dean Farm Shop,
Wickham Road, Fareham, Hants PO17 5BN.

Harvest Delicatessen,
46 West Street, Alresford, Hants SO24 9AY.

Hereford & Worcester
The Mousetrap,
1 Bewell Square, Hereford.

The Mousetrap,
3 School Lane, Leominster, Herefs HR6 8AA.

Isle of Wight
Benedict's Fine Wines and Delicatessen,
28 Holyrood Street, Newport, Isle of Wight PO30 5AU.

Kent
James's,
188 High Street, Beckenham, Kent BR3 1EN.

Lees Cheeses,
Northways, Burleigh Road, Charing, Nr Ashford, Kent TN27 0JB.

Perfect Partners,
7 Stone Street, Cranbrook, Kent TN17
3HJ.

Lancashire
The Ramsbottom Victuallers Co Ltd,
16-18 Market Place, Ramsbottom, Bury,
Lancs BL10 9HT.

Lincolnshire
Comestibles,
82 Bailgate, Lincoln LN1 3AR.

London
Barstow and Barr,
24 Liverpool Road, London N1.

Clarkes,
122 Kensington Church Street, London
W8.

James Elliott,
96 Essex Road, Islington, London N1.

Jeroboam's,
51 Elizabeth Street, London SW1.
Tel: 071-823 5623

Jeroboam's,
24 Bute Street, London SW7 3EX.
Tel: 071-225 2232

La Fromagerie,
62 Talbot Road, Highgate, London N6.

Mortimer and Bennett,
33 Turnham Green Terrace, London
W4.

Mr Christian's Provisions,
11 Elgin Crescent, London W11.

Neal's Yard Dairy,
17 Shorts Gardens, London WC2.
Tel: 071-379 7646

Paxton & Whitfield,
93 Jermyn Street, London SW1Y 6JE.
Tel: 071-930 0259

Mr C Roundell,
39 St Maur Road, London SW6.

The Cheeseboard,
26 Royal Hill, Greenwich, London SE10.

The Real Cheese Shop,
62 Barnes High Street, London SW13.

The Real Cheese Shop,
96A High Street, Wimbledon Village,
London SW19.

Villandry,
89 Marylebone High Street, London
W1.

Norfolk
The Mousetrap,
2 St Gregory's Alley, Pottergate,
Norwich NR2 1ER.

Northamptonshire
Essentially English, 10b West Street,
Oundle, Northants.

Northumberland
The Real Cheese Shop,
6 Oldgate, Morpeth, Northumberland
NE16 1LX.

Nottinghamshire
Cheese Cuisine,
10 Saracen's Head Yard, Newark, Notts NG24
1XA.

The Cheese Shop,
14 Market Street, Bingham, Notts NG13
8AB.

Whitewell's Delicatessen,
93a Melton Road, West Bridgford,
Notts.

Oxfordshire
Oxford Cheese Co,
17 Covered Market, Oxford OX1 1EF.

Wells Stores,
29 Stert Street, Abingdon, Oxon OX14
3JF.

Shropshire
Williams of Wem,
17 High Street, Wem, Salop SY4 5AA.

Somerset
The Cheeseboard,
10 Market Place, Wells, Somerset BA5
2RF.

The Cheese and Wine Shop
11 South Street, Wellington, Somerset.

Suffolk
The Cheese Shop,
74 Beccles Road, Oulton Broad,
Lowestoft, Suffolk NR33 8QY.

Surrey

Bentalls,
Wood Street, Kingston upon Thames,
Surrey KT1 1TX.

Brewery Court Ltd,
19 Kings Ride, Camberley, Surrey GU15
4HV.

Cheese World,
Milkhouse Gate, 142 High Street,
Guildford, Surrey GU1 3HJ.

La Charcuterie,
High Street, Cranleigh, Surrey GU6
8HZ.

Parsons Pantry,
12 Upper Church Lane, Farnham,
Surrey GU9 7PW.

Vivians,
2 Worple Way, Richmond, Surrey TW10
6DF.

Sussex

Horsham Cheese Shop,
20 Carfax, Horsham, West Sussex RH12
1EB.

The Cheese Shop,
17 Kensington Gardens, Brighton, East
Sussex BN1 4AL.

Say Cheese,
Gardner Street, Herstmonceux, East
Sussex BN27 4LE.

Say Cheese II,
Riverside, Lewes, East Sussex.

Warwickshire

Paxton & Whitfield,
13 Wood Street, Stratford-upon-Avon,
Warwicks CV37 6JF.
Tel: 0789 415544

West Midlands

Paxton and Whitfield,
3 Manor Walk, Solihull, Birmingham.

The Little Deli Co,
3 Belwell Lane, Mere Green, Sutton
Coldfield B74 4AA.

Yorkshire

The Cheeseboard,
1 Commercial Street, Harrogate, North
Yorks.

Lewis and Cooper,
92 High Street, Northallerton, North
Yorks DL17 8PP.

The Farm Dairy,
3 Market Place, Knaresborough, North
Yorks HG5 8AL.

The Food Emporium,
25a Front Street, Acomb, York YO2
3BW.

York Beer Shop,
28 Sandringham Street, York YO1 4BA.

Silver Hill Dairy,
105 Eccleshall Road, Sheffield, South
Yorks S11 9PH.

The Queens Kitchen,
2 Queens Court, Main Street, Bingley,
West Yorks.

WALES

The Farmhouse Cheese Shop,
Carmarthen   Provision   Market,
Carmarthen, Dyfed.

Howell's of Cardiff, 10-14 St Mary's
Street, Cardiff

Irma Fingal-Rock
64 Monnow Street, Monmouth, Gwent
NP5 3EN.

SCOTLAND

The Cheesemonger,
30A Victoria Street, Edinburgh EH1 2JN.

Valvona & Crolla,
19 Elm Row, Edinburgh EH7 4AA.

Glossary

Anybody who becomes interested in cheese and the methods by which it is produced is likely to come across at least some of the following terms.

Annatto — Natural, tasteless orange colouring from the seed of a West Indian tree. There is no substitute.

Bloom — A soft, downy mould which either occurs naturally on the surface of a cheese or is sprayed on.

Blue-veining — A blue mould, usually penicillium roquefortii or penicillium glaucum, is added to the milk or injected into the cheese. As the cheese ripens, the blue veining spreads.

Brine — A solution of salt and water in which cheese is soaked.

Buttermilk — The liquid that remains after cream has been turned into butter.

Casein — The main protein in milk which solidifies when it is coagulated.

Cheddaring — The stage in cheesemaking when curds are blocked and repeatedly stacked and turned to achieve maximum drainage.

Coagulation — The clotting of milk by the addition of either rennet or lactic acid.

Culture — A controlled production of micro-organisms.

Curds — The solid matter resulting from the formation of lactic acid in milk.

Curing — The ageing or ripening process of cheese.

Creamery — Factory where cheese is made on a large scale.

Enzymes — Parts of living cells which cause specific chemical changes according to the substances with which they come into contact.

Fermier — Term used to describe unpasteurised cheese produced traditionally on a farm.

Fresh — Unripened.

Homogenise — The treatment of milk so that the fat droplets are emulsified and the cream does not separate.

Ironing — Obtaining a sample from a whole cheese by inserting a cheese iron and extracting a core which is replaced.

Junket — Milk coagulated with rennet.

Lactation — The production of milk. The lactation period is the timespan between a mammal first producing milk after giving birth until the milk dries up.

Lactic — Often used to describe the smell and flavour of milk with regard to cheese.

Lactic Acid — The acid produced from the bacterial action on milk (souring).

Mould — Micro-organism which spreads over or through cheeses.

Moulds — Containers in which curds are placed to drain.

Paste — The interior of a cheese.

Pasteurisation — Heating milk to at least 72°C for a minimum of 15sec in order to destroy harmful micro-organisms; however, the process also destroys harmless, flavour-enriching micro-organisms.

Pathogens — Agents causing disease.

Pressed Cheeses — The curds have been pressed to release more whey during production.

Raw Milk — Milk which has not been heated or treated in any way.

Rennet — A preparation made from rennin, an enzyme in an unweaned mammal's stomach, which helps coagulate milk. Vegetarian rennet is either chemically produced or extracted from a number of flowers and plants.

Rennin — An enzyme found in the stomachs of unweaned mammals.

Scalding — The heating of the curds so that more whey can be extracted.

Skimmed Milk — Milk which has had some of the cream removed from it.

Starter — A bacterial culture of sour milk with a high concentration of lactic acid which is added to raw milk to increase its acidity.

Territorial Cheeses — Caerphilly, Cheddar, Cheshire, Derby, Double Gloucester, Lancashire, Red Leicester, Wensleydale.

Truckle — A small cylindrical cheese, usually weighing between 4 and 10lb.

Unpasteurised Milk — Raw milk which has not been heat treated.

Washed Rind — The cheese has been rinsed during ageing in liquids, including salt water, whey, beer, wine or oil, to inhibit the growth of moulds.

Whey — The clear liquid separated from the curds during cheesemaking. Often made into milk powder, and very nutritious.

Associations and Acknowledgements

Farmhouse Cheesemakers Ltd
(See page 53)
PO Box 457
Wells
Somerset BA5 1UX
Tel: 0749 670994

Milk Marketing Board of England and Wales
Thames Ditton
Surrey KT7 0EL
Tel: 081-398 4101

Specialist Cheesemakers' Association
The Association exists primarily to represent the interests of cheesemakers and to promote awareness and appreciation of British cheeses both throughout the trade and to the public. Anybody can become a member. More information about the Association can be obtained from:
PO Box 256A
Thames Ditton
Surrey KT7 0HR
Tel: 081-398 4101

The Stilton Cheesemakers' Association
The Association is now approaching its Diamond Jubilee, having been founded in June 1936 when a few far-sighted individuals recognised that if Stilton was to remain the King of English Cheese, it required protection.
There are only seven companies making Blue and White Stilton today and six of them belong to the Association. Two are farmers' co-operatives, largely using milk from their members' herds, which were founded in the early years of this century.
PO Box 11
Buxton
Derbys SK17 6DD
Tel: 0298 26224

Vegetarian Society
Parkdale
Dunham Road
Altrincham
Cheshire WA14 4QG
Tel: 061-928 0793

Note: all telephone numbers starting 0 will commence 01 from April 1995.

Acknowledgements

Thanks are due to the following for their help in the compilation of this book and the use of photographs: Handmade Cheese of Scotland; The Specialist Cheesemakers' Association; The Stilton Cheesemakers' Association; University of Reading Rural History Centre; Farmhouse Cheesemakers Limited; National Dairy Council.